BUCKINGHAM

MURIEL T. VERNON

and

DESMOND C. BONNER

ISBN 0 9501040 0 0

First published 1969.
Second Edition 1984.

Printed in Great Britain by
Grillford Ltd.
Milton Keynes.

From the Air—Buckingham 1968

(*Aerofilms Ltd.*)

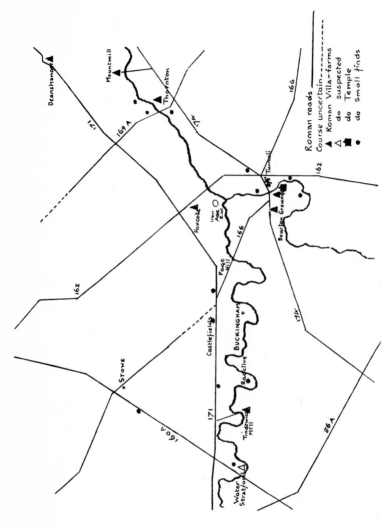

Roman Roads Around Buckingham (by the late C. W. Green)

CONTENTS

FOREWORD

BY

THE LORD LIEUTENANT OF BUCKINGHAMSHIRE, MAJOR J. D. YOUNG

BROWNE WILLIS and Lipscombe and, in the early part of this century, Harrison, have essayed histories of Buckingham and District and more impersonally there is the Victoria County History. And so it certainly seems appropriate that a new history should bring the story up to date.

It must be said that Buckingham has largely been by-passed by the main stream of history and by the XIXth century was a small country market town, perhaps rather dominated by the ducal house at Stowe. But what a wealth of local history lies behind this, in common no doubt with many other country towns. In the Middle Ages as a Prebend of Lincoln, the Church clearly had a great influence and after the Reformation, it is interesting to trace the municipal and political development of the Borough from its first Charter in 1554 granted by Queen Mary. Unlike most of the County, Buckingham supported the Royalist Cause in the Civil War, and the Great Fire of 1725 must have swept away much of the ancient Borough.

To anyone driving into the Town today, it is worth looking at the Swan placed on the roof of the Town Hall. This is the same Badge under which the men of Buckingham are reputed to have fought under Henry V at Agincourt in 1415—surely a visible link with the past.

ACKNOWLEDGEMENTS

WE would like to thank the many people who have helped in the preparation of this book. First to Miss G. Lawson, the former librarian at the Branch Library in Buckingham. Without her this book would not have been written, as she said that a short, easily read account of the history of Buckingham was needed, and suggested that we should write it. With her encouragement and the help of her staff in obtaining source material, the book has been written. Thanks also to the staff of the Buckinghamshire Reference Library at Aylesbury for the loan of books.

We are honoured that the Lord Lieutenant of the County, Major Young has consented to write the foreword.

For help with the original book we would like to thank the late Mr. Charles Green, the late Rev. J. H. B. Elkerton, then vicar of Buckingham and Mrs. D. J. Elkerton who was then mayor. Also Mr. A. Archdeacon, previously Town Clerk, Mr. D. C. Stewart, Mr. D. J. Elliott, Hon. Archivist to the Mayor and Corporation of Buckingham, the Buckinghamshire Archaeological Society, Mrs. E. M. Elvey, and the late Miss C. Baker, Mr. J. C. Jenkins, the late Sir Harry Verney, Mr. G. B. Clarke, the Rev. C. M. Devine, Mrs. E. Mason, the late Miss A. Palmer and the late Mr. B. A. Butler, Mrs. E. A. E. Middleton and Messrs. Lorimers.

We are grateful to Dr. C. R. Brown, Mr. G. W. Cantell and Mrs. P. Manning for information about Buckingham Hospital. We would like to thank Mr. P. R. Markcrow, General Manager of the Buckingham Borough Development Company, Mr. E. Evill, the last Town Clerk of Buckingham Borough and Councillor D. A. T. Foote who gave us information about the Development Company and other Buckingham matters.

We would also like to thank the Wipac Group, Leslie Hartridge Ltd., Cementone-Beaver Ltd. and Sigma Coatings Ltd. for their help.

Finally our thanks to Mr. K. C. Vernon who has read, checked, made suggestions, helped to arrange the index and encouraged us in many ways.

AUTHORS' REFERENCES

The following publications provided source material, and many are referred to in the text. Where an abbreviation is used instead of the full title, it is shown in brackets in this list.

" SOME ACCOUNT OF THE TOWN OF BUCKINGHAM " by Rev. H. Roundell, M.A. (Roundell).

" LEISURE-HOUR NOTES ON HISTORICAL BUCKINGHAM " by J. T. Harrison. (Harrison).

" THE VICTORIA HISTORY OF THE COUNTY OF BUCKINGHAM ". (V.C.H. Bucks).

" ANTIQUITIES OF BUCKINGHAM " by Browne Willis. (Browne Willis).

BUCKINGHAM ARCHAEOLOGICAL SOCIETY NEWS LETTER.

" RECORDS OF BUCKINGHAMSHIRE "—the Journal of the Architectural and Archaeological Society for the County of Buckingham. (R.O.B.).

" ROMAN ROADS OF THE S.E. MIDLANDS " by The Viatores. (' Viatores ').

" HISTORY OF THE COUNTY OF BUCKINGHAM " by George Lipscomb. (Lipscomb).

" HISTORY AND TOPOGRAPHY OF THE COUNTY OF BUCKINGHAM " by J. J. Sheahan. (Sheahan).

" ENCYCLOPAEDIA BRITANNICA ".

" THE DRAGON OF WHADDON " by J. G. Jenkins.

" THE BUCKINGHAM MINT " by Dolley, Elliott and Elmore Jones.

" THE ROYAL LATIN SCHOOL, BUCKINGHAM (CHAPEL OF ST. JOHN BAPTIST) " by J. T. Harrison.

" THE NEW BRITISH TRAVELLER, OR MODERN PANORAMA OF ENGLAND AND WALES " by James Dugdale.

" BUCKINGHAM TOWN, BUCKINGHAM PEOPLE AND THEIR NEIGHBOURS DURING THE CIVIL WARS " by Rev. H. Roundell.

" SOME NOTES ON THE EARLY HISTORY OF STOWE " by a member of the Sixth Form.

" THE BUCKINGHAMSHIRE MISCELLANY " by R. Gibbs. (Gibbs).

HILLIER'S ALMANACKS.

" THE BUILDINGS OF ENGLAND—BUCKINGHAMSHIRE " by Sir Nikolaus Pevsner.

" THE CHURCH BELLS OF BUCKINGHAMSHIRE " by A. H. Cocks, M.A.

" MEMOIRS OF THE VERNEY FAMILY " Volume IV, by Margaret M. Verney.

" THE VERNEYS OF CLAYDON " by Sir Harry Verney.

" ROYAL VISITS TO THE BOROUGH OF BUCKINGHAM " by Douglas J. Elliott, Hon Archivist to the Mayor and Corporation of Buckingham.

" THE NEW BOOK OF MARTYRS " by Rev. Henry Southwell.

" THE STOIC ".

PAPERS FORMERLY BELONGING TO J. T. HARRISON.

" THE UNIVERSITY COLLEGE AT BUCKINGHAM " by J. and J. Pemberton.

PAPERS FROM THE BUCKINGHAM BOROUGH DEVELOPMENT CO. LTD.

CHAPTER I

THE TOWN OF BUCCA'S PEOPLE

BUCKINGHAM today is a fairly typical Midland market town, with
a river winding among its houses, a church on a hill called Castle
Hill, its old brick town hall topped by a glittering swan, and
there is a castellated gaol in the middle of the main street. The
river and hill have had a controlling influence on the siting of the
town, and the buildings illustrate events in its history.

Primitive man, who built Stonehenge on Salisbury Plain has
left no such spectacular monuments around Buckingham. The
only evidences of his presence are a few flint implements from
Page Hill and Maids Moreton[1]. Bronze Age man also has left
little evidence; only a polished stone axe of Langdale origin, from
Shalstone[2], so perfect that it is suspected to have been for ceremonial
use only.

The history of England from 500 B.C. to 500 A.D. was dominated first by Celtic immigrants then by Roman invaders, who came
from Europe in a variety of craft and for varying reasons. From
500 B.C. the Celts began to come to England, being pushed out
of their homelands in the Rhineland by increasing population.
They settled fairly peacefully in the lowlands of the south and
east England, bringing their improved methods of agriculture,
including the two-ox plough and the iron ploughshare which enabled them to cope with more varied land.

Around 300 B.C. some warlike people from North France
and Brittany brought the more sophisticated La Tène culture across
to Britain. They spread across the country, mining iron on the Weald
and probably in Northamptonshire. Their smiths forged this iron
and bronze, which was still in use, into shields, horse armour,
swords and sheaths, flamboyantly decorated with fantastic plants
and animals (though not humans), and with geometrical designs.
They bred and traded horses and cattle, and grew wheat as a major
crop, which after the Roman occupation was even exported to
Rome. These people were at Hunsbury and a site near Olney, but
a different group, with a cruder type of pottery settled on high
ground to the north-east of Buckingham, around Leckhampstead
and Lillingstone[3].

The landscape at that time would be different from today. The
old idea was that in prehistoric times, rivers were wider and deeper,
with marsh on either side, and forest beyond this—an uninviting
place for people armed with only primitive tools. Mr. Charles
Green gives a different picture of our valley in those days; a wide
deep river with banks drier than today, as implied by the Iron

[1] [2] [3] Notes provided by C. W. Green.

Age and Roman houses which have been found in groups, under today's flood meadows at Emberton, near Olney, by the Nene at Billing, and at Felmersham in Bedfordshire. The climate was possibly warmer, as the Romans grew grapes in the open; the hills may not have been forested, as Iron Age and Roman sites have been found on the Ouse ridges where the Norman forests of Whittlewood, Salcey and Yardley Chase have been cleared. Some of these sites were extensive, and all agricultural, implying open country for grazing and corn growing.

Later in the Iron Age, possibly early 1st century B.C., a farm enclosure was established on a hillock near Hyde Lane Lakes, at the Twins—the joining of the two rivers, Padbury Brook and the Great Ouse. This enclosure consisted of a very deep ditch and rampart, inside which a large socketed iron axe, dated between 100 B.C. and 50 B.C., was found in 1965[4], while a corn-grinding quern was found in the gravel pit nearby. These people at Hyde Lane settlement may have been the immediate predecessors of the Belgic peoples, another group of Celts, who retreated from their homes in Gaul before the advancing Roman legions. These Belgic tribes crossed the Channel, bringing the art of the potter's wheel, a gold coinage and a currency of iron bars and ingots. Some iron no doubt was carried on the ancient trade track from the Nene ironstone quarries near Irchester which crossed Padbury Brook at Thornborough Bridge[5].

Markets were established in the south, town life was beginning and even the little settlement at Hyde Lane would be affected. Possibly it was overrun by the Belgic peoples, who with their superior culture would become the local aristocracy.

Roman Buckingham

The Belgic peoples who had been driven out of their homes by the Romans, kept sending help to their friends on the other side of the Channel, stiffening their resistance to the Romans.

By A.D. 43 an expansionist policy ruled Rome, while Britain was divided by tribal rivalries, some tribes violently anti-Roman, against others almost pro-Roman. The time was right for invasion. Aulus Plautius with a well equipped army of 40,000 men landed in Kent and advanced on London, then on the native capital, Camulodunum, now Colchester. Using these two towns as bases he proceeded to subdue England. Roads were built and garrison stations constructed in the conquered part, while the campaign continued further afield.

Within a few years everything south of the Humber and east of the Severn had been directly annexed or entrusted to native under-princes. The more difficult task of subduing the hill tribes

---

[4] Notes provided by C. W. Green. Axe found by Mr. G. Beckett. Details from Mr. W. Manning, Cardiff University.
[5] Notes provided by C. W. Green.

of Wales and Yorkshire came later. Large tracts of country—Ireland and Scotland—were untouched by the Romans, and Iron Age culture continued there uninterrupted at this time. In the highlands of northern England the Romans established only a military dictatorship, and even in the lowland zone of heavy occupation, the people remained basically Celtic throughout the occupation, and Iron Age traditions were preserved.

The Romans did not deliberately clear forested land for agriculture, but by driving roads through difficult country, much new land was opened up for settlement and farming.

There is no reliable evidence of Belgic resistance locally, and though men would be conscripted for construction work, normal life would be resumed soon after the Roman army swept northwards. Even the defendable Iron Age forts on high ridges overlooking the Ouse and Nene were not defended. Narbury on Whaddon, ' Danesborough ' on Brickhill and Hunsbury near Northampton were all by-passed by the invaders, or deserted by the defenders. Roman coinage and a Roman type economy were soon established. As new Roman sites are continually found, it is realised that the Belgae-British must have co-operated with the Romans, and the building of the towns and villas went on apace.

Although the town of Buckingham has no known Roman material beneath its streets, there have been many finds in the surrounding districts. There were many Roman roads around Buckingham, some of which have remained as foundations for modern roads, e.g. A.5 runs partly over the Roman Watling Street, which went through Magiovinium at Fenny Stratford, and Lactodorum at Towcester. A.421 from Buckingham to Bletchley often follows the line of a Roman road[6] which crossed the Ouse at Lockmeadow, then passed the Thornborough tumuli as it took course for Magiovinium.

Two roads ran roughly S.E. to N.W., parallel to Watling Street. One[7] follows an ancient pre-Roman road which may have been used by Claudius when subduing the country. It crosses the river at Thornton near the present bridge, then with an unexplained bend runs behind the chestnuts on the east side of the road leading to A.422. The other road[8] parallel to Watling Street apparently went from Roman buildings at Fleet Marston, north to Towcester, crossing the Bletchley road near the tumuli, and the river Ouse just east of the Hyde Lane Iron Age settlement.

A road ran on either side of the Ouse valley, on good soils above the river terraces, serving the villa settlements which were evenly spaced along the terraces. The road to the north of the river[9] served a villa at Tingewick, and an attached industrial building

[6] Road 166 on ' Viatores ' maps.
[7] Road 169 on ' Viatores ' maps.
[8] Road 162 on ' Viatores ' maps.
[9] Road 171 on ' Viatores ' maps.

thought to be a depot for dyeing and fulling, all flourishing between A.D. 260 and 400[10]. A Roman farm site at Castle Fields near this Roman road is suggested by finds of Rev. Roundell there in the last century[11].

The Belgic family who were farming near Hyde Lane would be overrun by the Romans, but these people possibly adapted themselves to the new government, and once Romanised, would keep their social position, with a well-built villa below Foscote, just above their old settlement. This was excavated in 1840[12], when a tesselated pavement was removed to Stowe, and is now set in the floor of the music room at the school. The baths for the villa were supplied by spring water carried through lead pipes, and the rooms heated by tiled flues. The villa would have outbuildings for slaves and farm animals, possibly around a central courtyard. The owners would be cultured people with Roman clothes and hair styles, and probably thought of themselves as Romans.

Possibly the owners of another settlement near Thornborough Bridge were even more important people, who had the two tumuli close to Thornborough as their burial monuments. One of these mounds[13], opened in 1839 by the Duke of Buckingham, was presumed robbed, but the other yielded an exciting and rich group of glass and bronze utensils and ornaments. Two bronze jugs, the smaller decorated with a lion's head, an oil lamp and some dishes, one decorated with a sea horse or bird, were found, as well as ashes and fragments of bone, preserved in a glass vessel, next to a piece of gold. The mounds are dated at about 180 A.D., and rows of skeletons reported near to the mounds point to an enclosed cemetery of a largish settlement[14]. A Roman house was on the Buckingham side of the bridge, and another near it on the ridge, close to the cottages at the gates to Bourton Grounds. Also near the river was a Romano-Celtic temple[15], facing across to the tumuli, and evidently associated with them. This was excavated in 1963-4, exposing a central sanctuary—the 'cella' of the god, probably a river god—surrounded by a veranda 57 feet square, with an entrance from the river side flanked by small chambers. Skeletal remains lay beneath the entrance, and over the floor near the god's seat were 315 coins ranging from A.D. 117 to A.D. 406, which had probably fallen through holes in the floorboards. The temple remained in use till long after the official adoption of the Christian faith by the Romans, and appears to have been at one time deliberately set on fire.

[10] Excavated by Roundell 1862. R.O.B. Volume 3, page 33.
[11] Sheahan page 28.
[12] R.O.B. Volume 5, page 355.
[13] R.O.B. Volume 16, page 29. The Thornborough Barrow, by Joan Liversidge, M.Litt., F.S.A.
[14] Notes provided by C. W. Green.
[15] R.O.B. Volume 17, page 356. A Romano-Celtic Temple at Bourton Grounds, by Charles W. Green.

The road on the south side of the Ouse[16] passes near to the tumuli, making this an important cross-roads of five different Roman roads.

Other villas served by these roads were at Thornton and Deanshanger, the latter being so important that the Roman road appears to have altered its course to skirt the villa, whose remains lie under the centre of Kingsbrook School sports field. This important road can be traced as far east as Cambridge.

Men from Spain, Syria and Greece were taken into the army to come to Britain and man the defences or be posted to garrison towns across the land. At the end of their service, not all of them returned to their home countries. Some were offered a piece of land in this country, where they could be demobilised and settle down as farmers. A pretty local girl would marry a Roman soldier with his own land. So a few of the Romans stayed on, but many returned to their homes on the continent at the end of their service.

Saxon Times

By 410 A.D. the continental empire was threatened by barbarians from the east, and the last Roman troops were withdrawn from many outposts of the empire to help in its defence. Britain was left to fend for herself, with Picts attacking from the north and Saxons raiding the south and east coasts. A few Saxons may have come at the invitation of the British, to help expel the Picts, and they may then have turned on their hosts. Many more came in raiding parties which developed into invasions, with a long period of warfare between the natives and the invaders, in which the latter steadily won a firmer hold.

The invaders gradually penetrated far inland, up the eastward flowing rivers such as the Great Ouse, using rivers as well as roads for their infiltrations. By about 500 A.D. all the eastern part of England at least as far north as the Humber was probably in Saxon or Anglo-Saxon hands. Apart from Kent taken by the Jutes from Jutland, the rest of the country was annexed by the strongest or the first there, whether Angles or Saxons. England was divided into many kingdoms, ruled by chieftains, the three principal ones being Northumbria in the North, Wessex in the south-east, both Saxon, and Mercia, a midland Anglian kingdom that included Buckingham. Intermittent warfare with varying fortunes and varying frontiers, continued between all these kingdoms for 300 years.

In 571 A.D. the Saxon King Cuthwulf of Wessex and his army swept across this countryside to subdue pockets of British who had escaped the initial onslaught[17]. He did not seem to maintain Saxon domination over this outer territory, for in A.D. 626 King Penda began his reign over the Angles of Mercia, including Buckingham.

[16] Road 174 on ' Viatores ' maps.
[17] V.C.H. Bucks, page 279.

13

He was an aggressive king, the last of the great heathen kings of Mercia, and he had a royal household at King's Sutton, between Banbury and Brackley. It was at King's Sutton that Penda's grandson Rumwold was born of Christian parents, probably rather later that 626, the date given by Browne Willis.

Ten Latin lines entitled " The Life of Rumwold, by an unknown author ", was transcribed by Bishop Grandison in 1336 and deposited in the Chapter records of Exeter Cathedral. Here is the translation:

> Rumwold's father was King of Northumberland[18].
> Rumwold's mother was a daughter of Penda, King of Mercia.
> Rumwold was born in the village of King's Sutton.
> Rumwold was baptised at Sutton by Bishop Widerin.
> Rumwold's godfather was the Presbyter Edwold.
> Rumwold lived only three days.
> Rumwold died upon the ninth of November.
> Rumwold was buried by Edwold in King's Sutton.
> The next year his body was carried by Widerin to Brackley.
> The third year after his death his remains were carried to Buckingham.

The mention of the name of our town is proof that before this time an Angle called Bucca had established a farmstead, probably at the defendable site within the loop of the river, at a place where good, firm ground came down on both sides of the river, which was fordable at this point.

At this time heathen and Christian customs were probably maintained side by side. Rumwold's fantastic story of a preaching babe who directed Buckingham to be his final shrine, contains a shred of historical sense in that the church at Buckingham remained subservient to that of King's Sutton almost to the Reformation, 800 years later. The baby Rumwold came to be considered as a saint. Several churches, wells and springs were dedicated to him, including at least one off Bath Lane, which was excavated by the Archaeological Society in 1968. His name is recalled by Rumbold's Lane, and he was among the few Anglo-Saxon saints to have maintained their place even after the Norman Conquest.

There was civil war almost continuously in England at this time, between provinces held down by ferocious princelings. Farm holdings and other property was in constant danger, and had to be protected by large or small fortifications. These fortified places or ' burgs ' account for many of our local names, the prefix sometimes being the owner's name, and sometimes connected with the position of the defended site. Local names include Padbury, Whittlebury, Westbury (west of Buckingham), Mixbury (the fort by the dunghill), Lenborough, Thornborough, Singleborough and Bourton, though Bourton's name may be connected with defences against the Danes.

[18] Roundell, page 2.

These Danish raids started in 789, when King Offa ruled Mercia, making it the dominant kingdom. Offa is believed to have had a palace at Winslow, and gave Winslow, with land in the Horwoods to St. Albans Abbey. During the next century the raids of the heathen Danes became invasions, the seafaring Danes penetrating particularly up the rivers that opened invitingly on the east coast. King Alfred of Wessex was forced to retreat to the marshes of the River Parret in Somerset, until he could gather an army and defeat his Danish adversary, Guthrum, at Edington. By the Peace of Wedmore that was then signed, the Danes were to retire to the east of Watling Street, as far south as Old Stratford, then along the Ouse to Bedford, and so down the Lea to the Thames. The principal Danish leaders were also forced to become Christian.

Alfred then set about organising his defences. He divided the country into shires, each under the local government of a ' burg ', which was a fortified town, often at an easily defendable site. Buckingham was in such a position, on the banks of the slow-moving Ouse, a river that would attract Danish invaders, and would need heavy defences. Also three Roman roads came from Danish-held territory through Buckingham and another Roman road from Towcester passed near the town. Buckingham needed to be held, and Alfred made it the capital of his new county[19].

The buildings of the town would be wooden huts and storehouses, surrounded by a wooden stockade; this tiny town may have been perched on top of Castle Hill, a naturally defendable position. The people living there were part of an almost democratic society. There were some slaves, but most people were freemen, not serfs, as real feudalism had not yet been introduced into Britain. Local matters were discussed and settled at the manor moot—an open meeting. The hundred moot and shire moot were for bigger districts and shires. The Witan, a council of Elders, advised and elected the king, usually the king's son being elected, but this was not always so.

Burghs were almost self-supporting; the produce of the town would be eaten or used by the people, with a little for trade. Crops were grown on strip fields, and forests in which pigs fed and wild animals roamed, surrounded the clearings. There were few stone buildings, as Roman methods had been forgotten. The Roman villas and towns were deserted ruins after raids and invasions by the Anglo-Saxons, who looked on them with awe, as buildings made in the past by a race of giants. The ruins were convenient quarries for stone, but as the Anglo-Saxons did not know how to build in stone, the stones were used for hearth, mill and altar stones until masons arrived from France and Rome to build stone churches and monasteries in late Saxon days.

The Treaty of Wedmore collapsed after a time, the Danes again went raiding, and Alfred's son, King Edward the Elder came to

[19] V.C.H. Bucks III, page 471.

Buckingham at Martinmas in 918, and stayed for four weeks while he supervised the building of two forts, one on each side of the river[20]. Their exact position is not known, but one may have been on Castle Hill and the other at Bourton—' Burgh-town '.

These forts, and the presence of the king, so impressed the Danes, that their Earl Thurkytel, with his captains and ' first men ' from Bedford, came to Buckingham to pay homage and surrender. Edward then re-occupied Bedford, the Danish resistance gradually collapsed, ending in 921 in a large-scale surrender to Edward at Passenham, where he was in residence. The forts of Buckingham had done their work, and in 934 the great King Athelstan[21], successor to Edward the Elder, visited the town and held a council here. The stockades of the forts would be mended and the houses tidied so that the king and his court would see Buckingham at its best, and when the court left, the shopkeepers would have had their busiest trading for years. King Athelstan decreed that every burgh should have a mint with a coiner working there. Buckingham mint[22] produced silver pennies, starting possibly at Michaelmas 973, some of which are in Stockholm and others in the British Museum.

The Danish settlers gradually became Christian, strong Saxon kings were recognised as overlords of England, until in 1000 Ethelred became king, and tried heavy bribery in the form of Danegeld, instead of strength to control the Danes. Then by killing the sister of Sweyn Forkbeard, King of Denmark, Ethelred precipitated the greatest attack by the Danes, when Sweyn in 1013 attacked and overran the country, plundering and burning all the way. Buckingham suffered a sacking in 1013, as it had in 1010, when it had been caught in a scythe-like sweep from the Thames, along the Ouse to Bedford. Our town, like the rest of the country was saved from further misery, only by the death of Sweyn in 1014, which was followed by four years of Ethelred, then a period of peace under Canute and his son, until 1042.

No coins have been found for the period while the country was ravaged by Sweyn, but the mint started work again early in Canute's reign and continued until 1060, the date of the last coin. The names of the moneyers were Tunulf, Sibwine, Aelfward, Leofric, Brihtwine, Leofwine and Aethelstan, and 36 of their coins remain. In the 85 years of operation the mint may have used about a ton of silver, which may have produced about 0.05% of England's coins of that period.

In 1042, after Canute and his son Harthacnut had died, the English nobles asked Edward the Confessor, the heir of the former throne of Wessex to come back as king of England. Edward had been brought up in the Norman court, and immediately tried to Norman-

[20] V.C.H. Bucks III, pages 471, 476. Sheahan, page 221.
[21] Royal Visits to the Borough of Buckingham, by Douglas J. Elliott.
[22] The Buckingham Mint, by Dolly, Elliott and Elmore Jones.

ise his English kingdom. He promised the throne of England to William, Duke of Normandy, when he died—which he had no right to do, as the king was elected by the Witan. William was delighted, as his dukedom of Normandy, while being independent of France, was not big enough for the ambitious descendant of Rollo the Viking.

Many English favoured Godwine, Earl of Wessex, then Harold, his son, as the future king, while Harold's brother, Tostig had hopes of his own. During the last years of his reign, Edward spent much of his time trying to complete the building of Westminster Abbey, leaving the organisation of his country to Harold Godwinson, who was therefore well trained for his work on the throne when Edward died. Harold, an able, tough, young Anglo-Saxon was ready for his short and eventful reign.

CHAPTER II

MEDIEVAL BUCKINGHAM 1066-1445

WILLIAM, Duke of Normandy was an ambitious man, the descendant of a Viking, and with a Viking's eyes for plunder which could be found in prosperous England. When Harold Godwinson accepted the throne of England, William knew that his only hope of winning England was by force of arms, so he set in motion the preparations shown on the Bayeux Tapestry. He was joined by his vassal lords and many landless knights—not all from Normandy—greedy for manors of their own, all followed by their men at arms.

Harold was defeated by William's army on October 14th on Senlac Hill near Hastings, and William, Duke of Normandy became King William 1st of England, being crowned on Christmas Day 1066 in Edward the Confessor's great new church—Westminster Abbey.

Much of the system of government in the country was changed by William. The feudalism that had become highly developed in France was introduced, and formed the basis for the holding of land and the relationships between the people. William held all the land of England—from God—though in effect he owned it. He leased the land, in large or small parcels to different people, nearly always Normans, and in return he was given an oath of allegiance and knight service; that is, the tenant would provide knights for the king in time of need. This tenant, usually a friend or relation of William, leased some of the land to other people, lower in the social scale, in return for allegiance, and either knight service that was handed down, or for work on the lord's land, or money. The one who leased the land was the vassal of the one above, and must swear to uphold his lord's interests. A chain of allegiances, duties, vassal and lord relationships was established, where duties were performed for rent for the use of land; the way was open for a great deal of oppression of the Anglo-Saxons by the Norman lords. William demanded feudal dues of two-thirds of the profits of the lands he leased, and also collected Danegeld. William very sensibly decided to keep a written record of all the land, corn mills, cattle, ship, pigs and people in England so that no-one would avoid taxation. This record is, of course, the Domesday Book.

Except on coastal or border country, William did not give any man control over a large district, but spread a man's holding over many counties, so that no man could become stronger than the king in any part of the country. He controlled the building of castles, having plenty for himself, manned by his own men, but not encouraging his earls to build their own castles in case they should defy him. To guard against tenants supporting their overlord in

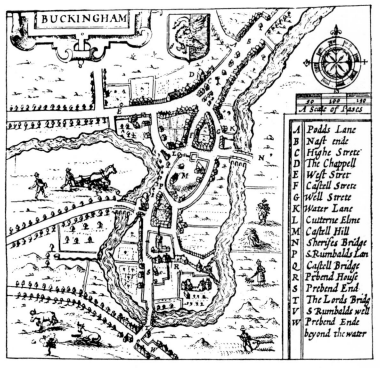

John Speed's Map of Buckingham—1610

Thomas Jeffrey's Plan of Buckingham—1770

defiance of the king, William had all tenants, great and small, swear allegiance to him, and to uphold him against his enemies.

William retained some of the Anglo-Saxon organisations; the courts—manor, hundred and shire—were kept, and the 'laws of Edward' were confirmed; this was a compliment to the Anglo-Saxon judicial system.

Buckingham at Domesday

These changes are illustrated by the condition of Buckingham at Domesday, when the little town of 27 burgesses had to pay the king £16 in silver, and was luckier than Aylesbury with £56 and £10 market toll, or Brill's £38 plus £12 'for the forest'[1].

The local manors were in Norman hands after the Conquest. Buckingham Manor, a Royal Manor, with which was included the borough, was assessed at one hide. (In Buckinghamshire areas of land were measured in carucates, while the liability to tax was expressed in hides, both hides and carucates varying in extent with the type of land[2]). Shortly after Domesday it was granted to Walter Giffard, Lord of Longueville in Normandy, son of an earlier Walter Giffard who was a cousin of the Conqueror. He was an important man, holding 48 manors in Buckinghamshire and some in other counties, and was probably granted Buckingham manor when he was created Earl of Buckingham by William's son, William II[3]. At Domesday, Walter Giffard already held Bourton Manor, which continued to be held with Buckingham manor till the 16th century.

Another manor at Bourton had been held by Alric, a thegn under Edward the Confessor, but at Domesday was held by Walter Giffard, with Hugh as his tenant. Later, Fulk de Bourton then Elia Fouk held the manor, but records ceased in 1399. Lenborough Manor also belonged to Walter and was assessed at three hides, more than Buckingham or Bourton. Walter's tenant at Lenborough was Ralph, and the previous tenant had been Towi, a man of Alric, son of Goding. Another manor at Lenborough had been held by Wilaf, a man of Earl Leofwine, an Anglo-Saxon, but in 1086 it was held by Odo, Bishop of Bayeux, a half-brother of the Conqueror, whose tenant was Ernulf de Hesding. In 1202, this manor, or part of it was acquired by Reading Abbey, part of the rent being in the form of payment for castle-guard at Rochester. The abbey held it till the Dissolution, when the abbot received an annuity of £3 3s. 4d. from Lenborough.

Prebend End Manor, alias Buckingham with Gawcott[4] was part of the endowment of Buckingham church, and in Edward's reign had been held by Ulf or Wolfin, Bishop of Dorchester on the Thames, but after he died in 1067 the Conqueror made Lincoln

[1] Notes provided by C. W. Green. V.C.H. Bucks I, page 221.
[2] R.O.B. Volume 16, page 342, Buckinghamshire in 1086, by G. R. Elvey.
[3] V.C.H. Bucks III, page 480-487.
[4] V.C.H. Bucks III, page 482. Sheahan, page 224.

the seat of the bishop, endowed it with Prebend End Manor and Buckingham church, and made his friend Remigius de Feschamp the first Bishop of Lincoln. This diocese of Lincoln was to become very big indeed, including land in Oxfordshire, Berkshire and Buckinghamshire.

Stowe Manor also passed from Saxon hands. Before the Conquest it was held by Turgisus, a man of Baldwin, the son of Herlwin[5], but in 1066 it was granted to Odo, Bishop of Bayeux. Odo was thrown into prison on a charge of disloyalty in 1082, and in 1088 the manor of Stowe was taken from him and granted a few years later to his tenant, Roger d'Oyley who made it part of the church which was in his castle grounds at Oxford, and which was part of Osney Abbey. Stowe remained the property of Osney Abbey until just before the Dissolution of the Monasteries[6].

So all the land around Buckingham was in possession of Normans who spoke a different language and held their Saxon tenants as feudal vassals. These three Normans had supported the Conqueror by providing ships for the Conquest. Odo promised 100, Walter Giffard 30, and Remigius one ship which held 20 knights. Life was not happy for the Anglo-Saxons; serfdom increased, there were fewer freemen, and no-one actually owned his own land. Land was leased from the Earl of Buckingham or the Bishop of Lincoln, and work had to be done on the landlord's manor to pay for the rent. Little time would be left for farming one's own lands, particularly at harvest time when the lord's land needed so much attention. Life was hard for the local Anglo-Saxons, and there would be little compensation in the fact that the Norman landlords were very important people; both Giffard and Remigius were friends of the Conqueror, and both appointed as commissioners for the survey of the Midland counties for the Domesday Book. That book was hated and feared, as the record grew of the number of hides of land, who held it, what livestock he owned, what it was worth, what rent and taxes, how much ploughland, and whether the man was a freeman, slave, cottager or villein. Not even secrets were left for the Anglo-Saxons, a conquered people.

Buckingham Manor

Walter Giffard, the first Earl of Buckingham possibly never lived in Buckingham, as this was a small and insignificant place for such an important man, and he held so many other manors elsewhere. Possibly if William permitted it, he built a castle here, on Castle Hill, or one may have been built after his death in 1102. Walter's son, Walter, second Earl of Buckingham lived through the reign of Henry I, a time of peace, when a strong king held his nobles in place, and when the Exchequer system of tax accounting started. He also would see the civil war in Stephen's reign, the type

[5] Lipscomb II, page 84.
[6] Early History of Stowe, by a Member of the Sixth Form. *The Stoic*—The History of Stowe—II.

of baron's revolt that the Conqueror had feared. He died in 1164, six years before Thomas a Becket was murdered, and as he was childless, his title of Earl of Buckingham is generally said to have died with him, and remained lapsed for over 200 years, until 1377. Walter's lands were held by Henry II, who doubtless was glad of the revenue, but Richard I on his accession in 1189, split Walter's lands between two of Walter's relations[7], the lands in Normandy going to William Marshal, Earl of Pembroke, and the lands in England to Richard de Clare (said by the *Encyclopaedia Britannica* to have held the title of Earl of Buckingham), both descendants of the sister of the first Earl of Buckingham.

Richard de Clare was overlord of the district and held this land and other manors directly from the Crown. When his daughter married William de Braose in 1215, her father granted her Buckingham as a dower, the manor remaining in the de Braose family until 1325. The overlordship then stood between the manor and the Crown, and was held from the 13th to the 16th centuries by the Earls of Gloucester and Stafford, who represented the Giffard Honour or Honour of Gloucester, the original direct holders of the land[8].

The story of William de Braose junior, son-in-law of Richard de Clare is confused. By combining various accounts, it seems that William's father was one of the barons who rebelled against King John, who in revenge, starved William and his mother to death in Windsor Castle. By this time William had a son, John, who was brought up in Wales by his Uncle Giles, Bishop of Hereford, out of the way of the vengeful King John. While in Wales he met and married Margaret, daughter of Llewellyn, Prince of Wales, and granted her Buckingham Manor as a dower. When John de Braose died in 1232, a man called Peter de Rivali was appointed as guardian of his two sons, William and Richard. Margaret, their mother, seems to have refused to hand over the children, and the king took possession of Buckingham Manor, granting it to Peter de Rivali until Margaret became more obedient. This type of pressure was often put on widows who owned land; they could also be forced to marry men they disliked on threat of having their land taken away.

Margaret[9] was a woman of character. She married again and her husband may have helped her to regain her land for her children; for though her son William was responsible for a debt of his father's in 1245, he did not obtain full possession of the manor until 1259, when his mother surrendered all claim to it in return for £40 a year. In 1254-5 Margaret's husband held some land in Bourton in the right of his wife, who he may have helped to win back her own land.

[7] V.C.H. Bucks III, page 480. Lipscomb II, page 549.
[8] V.C.H. Bucks III, page 480.
[9] V.C.H. Bucks III, page 480. Lipscomb II, page 558.

Buckingham Castle and Town

By this time Buckingham Castle was almost certainly built[10]: in 1279 Margaret's son, William de Braose held 3 carucates of land in demesne with a free fishery, all under the heading of 'castle' in the Buckingham records, and in 1305 Giles de Braose, his son, died in possession of a 'capital messuage called the Castle of Buckingham, worth nothing'. It sounds rather as though Buckingham Castle had been quickly built and as quickly fallen into disrepair. We know very few facts about Buckingham Castle and the only documentary records seem to be these:—in 1280 a man called Elias de Camvil was Constable of Buckingham Castle; in 1307 and 1312 Buckingham Castle is in the list of those to be defended and victualled; in 1453 the site of the castle was leased to Thomas Smythe; in 1473 the accounts of the manor include the cost of tiles, pins, nails, etc. needed to repair the cook's chambers, stables and 'le Garet' in the castle: in 1484 Richard III made a grant to John Grey of Wilton of certain moneys 'for the food for the King's hawkes secured upon the Castle and Manor of Buckingham', and in an old volume of Corporation Records there was an entry of Constable of Buckingham Castle in 1599.

At any rate, by the 13th century we seem to have had a castle which looked down upon a busy and prosperous town—the county town. The sheep on the limestone lands to the north, the eastern extension of the Cotswolds, produced wool on which much of our prosperity was based. Wool would be sold to the continent— especially Flanders—for weaving, though some cloth was sold in Buckingham, as shown by Richard le Marchand and Richard le Marcier, who in 1228 were fined for selling cloth contrary to the assize or measurement[11].

There was a hospital for lepers, dedicated to St. Laurence in Buckingham in the 13th century, though one would expect such a hospital to be outside a town. It is mentioned in 1252, when protection was granted to the master and brethren, and in 1312 the Bishop of Lincoln granted an indulgence to the lepers. The hospital had some endowments, but it seems that these were not sufficient, as in 1337 the master and brethren complained that they 'could not subsist' on them. The king then gave Gilbert de Buckingham, who lived in the town, a license to endow the hospital with lands and rents, and for a chaplain to 'celebrate divine service for the good estate of the king and the said Gilbert for ever'. It is not known when the divine services ceased, but records of the hospital disappear after the 14th century[12].

In the 12th century William Frechet built a hospital for the poor and infirm and dedicated it to St. John. John de Braose, William's

---

[10] Sheahan, page 227. Lipscomb II, page 570. V.C.H. Bucks III, page 476. Harrison, pages 11, 41. Browne Willis, pages 48, 49.

[11] V.C.H. Bucks III, page 471.

[12] V.C.H. Bucks III, page 486. Lipscomb II, page 583. Sheahan, page 240.

overlord, gave permission for the hospital to be built after the event; later it ceased to be a hospital, and John's steward took possession of the building. There must have been a lot of disappointment when the hospital failed, and the building was sold to Peter of the Mill, who was living in 1229. When Peter died it passed to John of the Mill, who sold it to Ernald de Ferur. He sold the building and 10 acres of land to Matthew de Stratton, Archdeacon of Buckingham, who converted it back to a hospital, the master of the hospital holding 1 acre of land in Moreton in 1279.

Matthew Stratton later gave the hospital to the master of the house of St. Thomas of Acon (St. Thomas a Becket) in London, who converted it into a chapel and chantry, and in 1289-90 obtained a licence to transfer his property in Buckingham to the Knights Hospitallers. This property included the hospital, and land given by various people—a carucate, 40 acres of land and 40s. rent. The building continued as a chapel until the Dissolution of the Monasteries, but before that it became dilapidated and was partially rebuilt by Archdeacon Ruding between 1471 and 1481. This is the building now known as the Old Latin School[13].

Chetwode Rhynde

It is said that in 1244 an enormous wild boar terrorised the neighbourhood of Chetwode, which is five miles south-west of Buckingham, and was then forested. Ralph de Chetwode found and fought the boar for four hours, and killed it; in gratitude he was granted the Chetwode Rhynde Toll. This gave the lord of the manor the right to levy, for one week each year, a tax on all cattle and swine passing through a district including Chetwode, Tingewick, Preston, Hillesden, Cowley, Gawcott, Lenborough and Prebend End in Buckingham. The accounts of the tax vary. Harrison says it was a farthing a claw, Sheahan 2s. a score on cattle and swine, and Gibbs 6d. per head on cattle, 5d. per head on sheep and pigs, being the correct tax, with 2s. a score as the one usually used. Local farmers could pay 1s. per year for immunity from the toll.

The toll was collected every year till 1875, when the coming of the railway and its use for the movement of stock had made the collection of the toll financially unrewarding. The toll started at mid-day on 29th October and continued for a week till mid-day on 7th November, a horn made of a conch shell being blown to mark the start, and the tax being collected by men placed at strategic points on the roads. At one time £20 was collected, but in later years the amount was less and the collection was organised by ' Cockey Giles ', Superintendent of the Borough Gaol, who collected a band of boys on Church Hill, blew the horn and distributed ginger bread and beer to them, then walked through Tingewick to the boundary with Oxfordshire, distributed more food, blew

[13] V.C.H. Bucks III, page 486.

the horn and said the toll had begun. The boys collected what they could.

The story of the reason of the toll sounds fantastic, but when a large mound near Tingewick Wood was levelled in 1810, the skeleton of an enormous boar was found; the teeth and jawbone were sent to Sir George Chetwode to be mounted and put in a glass case.[14]

Buckingham Manor Later

The manors of Buckingham and Bourton continued in the de Braose family at least until 1325, when John de Braose and his wife Sara settled two-thirds of Buckingham Manor on Robert Spigurnell, the other one-third being retained by Mary, a widow of William de Braose, probably John's mother. In 1328 John complained that someone had broken his tumbrel on his own land, had felled trees and assaulted his servant, but by 1335 things were happier, when he granted a shop in the High Street to Peter Dove the tailor and his wife Lora.

John's daughter, Elizabeth married John Frome, who held the manor in 1399. When John Frome died he left 100s. to the natives of Bourton, and Buckingham Manor passed to his daughter, who was soon widowed and left with two girls, the younger only four days old. Her second husband, John Cheyne handled the property, and his son, William, in 1446 released all right to the manor, to Robert Heworth and Robert Marshall, who had been involved in an earlier conveyance.

During this time, the title of Earl of Buckingham had been revived. Thomas of Woodstock, Duke of Gloucester, 6th son of Edward III was created Earl of Buckingham in 1377 at the coronation of Richard II. He was murdered at Calais in 1398. It seems that this man was the overlord of Buckingham Manor[8]. He was succeeded in the title by his son, Humphrey Plantagenet, who died childless in 1401, three years after his father. Humphrey was succeeded by his sister Anne Plantagenet, a countess in her own right, who married Edmund Stafford, Earl of Stafford. Their son, Humphrey Stafford became Earl of Buckingham on the death of his mother[15].

On 14th September, 1445 Humphrey Stafford, Earl of Stafford, was made Duke of Buckingham and was given precedence over all the other dukes in England and France, except royal dukes. This was the time of the 100 Years War, after the death of Joan of Arc, and when Henry VI was betrothed to Margaret of Anjou, niece of Charles VII. The precedence over dukes in France was not very significant, but in England the Duke of Buckingham stood high in the land. His precedence over all non-royal dukes brought him trouble with Henry Beauchamp, Duke of Warwick, to whom

[8] V.C.H. Bucks III, page 480.
[14] Harrison, page 88. Sheahan, page 267. Gibbs, page 285.
[15] Encyclopaedia Britannica—Earls, Marquesses, Dukes of Buckingham.

the king had unwisely given a similar privilege ! It needed a special Act of Parliament to settle the matter, and in the end it was arranged that the two dukes should take precedence by turns, one the first year, the other the next year and so on while both lived. When one died, the survivor would have precedence over the dead man's heir, but the heir who came into his inheritance first, should have precedence over the other's heir.

The Duke of Warwick died three years later, without any children, and on 22nd May, 1447, the Duke of Buckingham obtained a second grant to himself and his heirs, of rank over all dukes except those of the Blood Royal. In 1446 Humphrey Stafford, Duke of Buckingham obtained the Manor of Buckingham from Robert Heworth and Robert Marshall and brought together once more the overlordship or seignory and the possession of the manor. (This is some years before Lipscomb thinks that this happened, as he says that the overlordship and the mesne manor remained separate till ' both became vested in the Crown, in the time of Henry VIII'.)

With such an important man connected with the town, Buckingham's prosperity seemed assured.

Castle House

In the 14th century the Barton family were accumulating considerable property in Buckingham. William Barton in 1385 acquired the lands of William Goddes, and between 1398 and 1403 his sons (both apparently called John), John Barton sen. and jun. obtained other grants of land. This property was known as Barton's or Lambard's[16] and at one time was large, though later was reduced to the family house, Castle House and some acres of land. Until 1974 this house was the offices of the Borough Council.

John Barton sen., was, according to Browne Willis, in the time of Richard II and Henry IV, ' one of the Knights of the Shire in Parliament '. His will is quoted at length by Browne Willis, and shows with what care this man dealt with his property. Many small amounts of money were left to religious bodies, including £16 13s. 4d. for 4,000 masses to be said immediately after his death for his soul, and 6s. 8d. to ' a Person to see them faithfully performed '. Other legacies were left to the Master and Brethren of the Hospital of St. Thomas in London, and of St. Bartholomew's Hospital, the Abbot and Convent of Biddlesden, Prior and Convent of Luffield, Chetwode, Snellshall, Friars of Northampton, Oxford, Aylesbury and London, all to celebrate mass for his Soul and the Souls of his Father and Mother, Benefactors and Friends, and all the 'Souls of the Faithful departed.'

He left some property to his brother, John Barton jun. on condition that he find a chaplain to say daily mass at St. James's altar in the church at Buckingham. He gave detailed instructions

[16] V.C.H. Bucks III, page 484. Lipscomb II, page 568. Harrison, page 75. Sheahan, page 232. Browne Willis, pages 51, 54.

about the duties and payments of the chaplain, who was under the direction of the Master and Brethren of Thomas Becket's Hospital in London (who controlled the chantry chapel, later to become the Latin School, in Buckingham), and not the Bishop of Lincoln. His brother was to have a lamp burning day and night before St. Rumbold's shrine, and there were instructions about the size and weight of candles to be burned at the head and feet of St. Rumbold's sepulchure.

John Barton jun. ' shall find 6 poor Men or Women of the Town of Buckingham to pray daily for his Soul and the other Souls aforementioned, and that he shall give to each of them four Pence every week, and provide each of them a Mansion as he hath appointed them '. This was the start of Barton's Hospital in Church Street.

After John Barton jun.'s death, the property was to go to sisters Margaret and Isabel for their lives, then to William Fowler and his heirs, and if this line failed, to John Somerton then to William Purfrey.

A Royal Visit

On the 21st July, 1318[17], King Edward II was at Northampton, and by the 23rd he was at Woodstock, to the north-west of Oxford. Buckingham is on the route between the two places, and an entry in the Close Rolls suggests that the king stopped here at least for a meal. The entry says, ' To the Sheriff of Buckingham Order to pay Adam de la Haye of Buckingham 102s. 6d., which the King owes him for bread bought from him for the expenses of the King's household in July last, as appears by a bill under the seal of Roger de Norburgh, Keeper of the Wardrobe, in his possession'. At least one shopkeeper was better by 102s. 6d. for the visit, and the whole town would have something to talk about for the next few months.

Buckingham was thriving, busy with trade and also a place for fun. Then as now there were fairs in the town[18], the tolls going to the lord of the manor until the 16th century when they became part of the corporation revenues. In 1327 one-third of their value was said to be 13s. 4d., and in 1473 16s. 2½d. is in the accounts of Buckingham Manor, when stalls were rented at 4d. to 16d., and two spaces in the market were for the sale of fish.

The wool trade was still important, and though Buckingham was not one of the Staple Towns appointed by statute in 1353, we did have a wool or drapers' hall in the market place indicating that we were a centre for a local industry. Wool was sold and also woven in Buckingham, as shown by the license obtained by two Flemish weavers, Nicholas and Gervase Webb in 1436[19].

[17] Royal Visits to the Borough of Buckingham, by Douglas J. Elliott.
[18] V.C.H. Bucks III, page 479.
[19] V.C.H. Bucks III, page 471.

At about this time the cordwainers are mentioned in some accounts. Five shoemakers and four tanners all held stalls in the market-place at a yearly rent of 12d. each, the stalls being grouped together, a sign that they formed part of a craft-guild.

Buckingham was developing as a small though busy market town. The powerful overlords affected the history of the town in many ways; trade would be brought by these important people, but many town affairs would be controlled by them, sometimes to the benefit of the townsfolk but sometimes not. Their influence seems to have saved Buckingham some money in one way. In 1295 when the Model Parliament was called, representatives were sent for from other places in the county, but not from Buckingham, the county town. This could have been achieved through influence in high places, as in medieval times men were anxious to escape the financial and social responsibility of being called to Parliament, and a borough which managed to evade representation avoided paying its members and also paid less in taxation, as a borough represented only by Knights of the Shire was taxed less than one with its own representatives. As parliaments were called only to grant the king money, and were dissolved before their members' grievances could be heard, the clever people kept away.

In 1353 the Sheriff sent a precept to Buckingham to send a representative to parliament, but none was sent, nor to any medieval parliament.

Our position as a trading town had its drawbacks. In Edward III's time, Buckingham received two precepts to send representatives to the ' King's Councils in Matters relating to Trade '. The first one in 1337 was very strictly worded, and had to be obeyed, so three men were sent, Hugh Kynebell, Roger le Draper and Henry Selveston. The second precept seems to have been less commanding and was not obeyed—Buckingham was not represented at that ' Council in Matters relating to Trade '.

In the next few years[20] there was a blight of crops in the district and a fatal disease of cattle that was particularly severe in the Buckingham and Banbury area. This was followed in 1348 by the Black Death, of which Camden reports from an older record that at Luffield Priory, across the road from Silverstone Race Track, ' the Prior and all the monks died from the Great Pestilence '.

Although Buckingham was the county town, during the 13th and 14th centuries the assizes were held at Newport Pagnell for the northern hundreds, and at High Wycombe for the Chiltern district, and occasionally at Aylesbury or other places. Prisons were at Wycombe and Aylesbury in the reigns of Edward I, II and III, and at Aylesbury in the reign of Henry IV and in 1534. In that year there was a prison in Buckingham[21] Castle, which may have been used for this purpose since the time of Henry VI.

[20] Biddlesden and its Abbey, by C. W. Green, page 22.
[21] V.C.H. Bucks IV, page 525.

For many centuries the county had two centres, Aylesbury and Buckingham, with Wycombe as a third important place for assizes and administration. The process of making Aylesbury the official county town was only gradual, and was opposed by Buckingham.

Ecclesiastical History

Even before the Conquest, the church of Buckingham had been connected with that of King's Sutton (Sutton Regis); Browne Willis thought that there might have been one continuous parish including the two places, with Sutton as the ecclesiastical superior. If this was so, the intermediate parishes became independent, but Buckingham remained ecclesiastically connected with King's Sutton at the time of the Conquest. When Remigius de Feschamp was made Bishop of Lincoln, part of his diocese was divided into prebends, each administered by a prebendary who was a canon of the cathedral. Buckingham was in the prebend of Sutton-cum-Buckingham, with Horley and Horton; the revenues of this land supported the prebendary of the same name, who supplied curates or chaplains for the chapels of Buckingham, Horley and Horton. Richard de Gravesend is the first prebendary to be found in any of the past historical accounts of Buckingham. He was made Prebendary of Sutton-cum-Buckingham in 1265, and must have been very able, or had some influence as he was made Bishop of London in 1280. There may have been other prebendaries before this time, but they are not known.

Some of these prebendaries were extremely wealthy, important and influential men, with money which came from the rents of church lands and tithes. The prebend of Sutton-cum-Buckingham was the best endowed of any in Lincoln cathedral, and only one other in all England was wealthier.

The prebendaries of Sutton-cum-Buckingham were therefore even wealthier than the other prebendaries, and could pay other men to perform their church duties. They often lived abroad, and some even were foreigners, acting as absentee landlords for the lands they administered. Cardinal Neapolio was prebendary from 1303-1342 according to Lipscomb, though the Victoria History says that in 1298 the Abbot of Biddlesden was resigning the chapel of Buckingham (which he had leased for a term of years) into the hands of the cardinal's proctor. The cardinal seems to have lived abroad much of the time, enjoying the proceeds of his prebend. In 1323 there was excitement in Buckingham when the bailiffs arrested Richard le Kerdyf who had robbed Neapolio's proctor of £25 12s. The cardinal seems to have suffered quite a lot from robbery, as in 1327 John le Buckingham was said to have assaulted his servants, and in 1331 a cart laden with his tithe corn from Lenborough and Bourton, 160 lambs worth £20, and 40 swine worth 100s., from Gawcott were carried away. The cardinal resigned his stall in 1342 and lived another five years on the profits.

There must have been strong feelings about foreign absentee prebendaries, as in 1351 Edward III made an edict that no foreigners should hold high ecclesiastical posts. Despite this, Peter, Cardinal of St. George was prebendary in 1388 and Henry, Cardinal of Naples in 1389[22].

A change in the organisation of the prebend occurred in 1445, when the church of Buckingham became a vicarage and was therefore more independent. At the same time Horley and Horton were given a vicarage. This involved a rearrangement of the finances of the prebend. Walter Giffard, the first Earl of Buckingham had been lord of Longueville and had founded the Priory of Newton Longueville as a cell to St. Faith's at Longueville near Rouen. He made a grant of the tithes of his lands in Buckingham to the Priory of Longueville,[23] and this grant had been confirmed by Henry I, by William Marshal, Earl of Pembroke in 1150 and by a general charter of confirmation by Henry II in 1155. It seems that Cardinal Neapolio had the tithes in his own hands (unless he was collecting it for Longueville) in 1331 when someone robbed him of them. When the vicarage of Buckingham was instituted the tithes were divided, the greater tithes, that is the tithe on corn, hay and wood going to the prebendary, who was the rector, and the lesser tithes to the vicar.

Prebend End Manor was retained by the prebendary but a 'croft called Walnut Yard' or the field of walnuts, was given to the vicar, for the church, possibly as a site for a house, and is where the present vicarage stands. In 1445 this was not yet built, and the vicar presumably would live in the Manor House, which was the Prebend House (now with a twisted chimney) probably being occupied by the incumbent at Buckingham, as the prebendary would be too important a person to live there.

[22] V.C.H. Bucks III, page 483.
[23] V.C.H. Bucks III, page 487.

CHAPTER III

TROUBLED TIMES 1445-1554

HENRY VI was a gentle, quiet person who suffered from occasional attacks of insanity. The government of England and the direction of the current part of the 100 years war against France were not in his hands. For a while the war went well for us, and by 1429 we held most of France north of the Loire. Then the French soldiers, given fresh courage by the leadership of Joan of Arc, fought back and regained most of their country.

In the fourteen thirties, the Council who had control of the king's affairs quarrelled among themselves; some supported a more vigorous continuation of the war with France, until the whole country could be reconquered. The other party felt that to continue the war was a waste of time, lives and money. In 1444 there was a truce in the fighting. In an effort to settle the war, the group wanting peace, arranged that the king should marry Margaret of Anjou, who, being energetic, strong-minded and fond of her country, wanted peace between England and France. The Duke of York, descendant of Edward III, headed the party keen on beating France and regaining some of the land lost since Agincourt. According to Michael Drayton, men from Buckingham fought there:—

> The mustered men for Buckingham are gone
> Under the swan, the arms of that old town.

The animosity between the Duke of York and the French wife of the Lancastrian Henry VI, was the background to the start of the Wars of the Roses. The weakness of the king and the quarrels of the ruling council had produced a situation where important nobles had their liveried retainers in such numbers, as to be in effect, private armies.

In 1453, the king, who had always been weak, became quite mad, giving the Duke of York the opportunity to rule the country as 'Protector of the Realm'. A year later the king recovered enough to allow Margaret to regain control over the government; the York regency ended and York realised that he would have to fight for his rights and probably his life. He gathered his supporters and the long intermittent fighting and uneasy peace which was called the Wars of the Roses began.

Humphrey Stafford, Duke of Buckingham, who had precedence over all non-royal dukes, supported the king, and so did his son Humphrey. Humphrey junior was killed in the first fighting—a skirmish in the streets of St. Albans in 1455. His father was killed at Northampton on July 10th, 1460, when the Lancastrians were defeated. Henry Stafford, born 1454, before his father's death, was left without father or grandfather, and in consequence Edward IV, the new Yorkist king made Henry and his brother Humphrey royal wards. Henry would be six or seven years old, and for several years he and his brother lived in the Queen's household, grandsons of Lancastrians being brought up in a Yorkist palace. Henry Stafford was a direct descendant of Edward III, the owner of vast lands in central England, a person to be persuaded to the Yorkist cause. He was married to the queen's sister, Catherine Woodville, in order to tie him more closely to the Yorkist king, but he took little part in public affairs during Edward's reign, so probably was not trusted.

When Edward IV died, his brother Richard was appointed Protector for Edward's son, Edward V, a boy of 12. The Duke of Buckingham saw the way the land lay and came to London as Richard's chief supporter. He arranged the seizure of Edward V and his brother, denied their legitimacy because of an alleged previous marriage between Edward IV and Lady Eleanor Butler, and asked Londoners to declare Richard as King.

Richard III rewarded the duke with honours and lands. Buckingham served as Great Chamberlain at Richard's coronation, became Chief Justice in Wales, keeper of the royal castles in Wales and the border counties, steward of the honour of Tutbury, sole heir of the Bohun family (he was descended from Thomas of Woodstock and Eleanor Bohun). He also became Constable of England. Buckingham was as important as any man could be—anyone except the king. From April to July 1483 he supported Richard and received his rewards, but the next month he was at Brecon in Wales, plotting to replace Richard by putting Henry Tudor on the throne. The reason for the change of sides is not known, but he may have wanted the crown for himself, or his father's, grandfather's and uncle's deaths as Lancastrians may have been remembered bitterly. Possibly he did not completely trust Richard or could not accept the imminent murder of the two young Princes in the Tower. At any rate he was ready to support a revolt that was to begin on October 18th, 1483; but a week before that, Richard declared that Buckingham was a traitor. His troops disappeared, he was captured at Wem in Shropshire and taken to Richard at Salisbury, where he was beheaded on Sunday, November 2nd in the market place[1].

His lands were taken by the King, who, according to Browne Willis, granted Buckingham Manor to Richard Fowler, Chancellor of the Duchy of Lancaster, who at that time owned Castle House. This is doubtful, as according to the Victoria History, Vol 3, page 484, in 1483 when the Duke of Buckingham was beheaded, Richard Fowler was dead, and Castle House was owned by his son, Edward.

When Richard III died on Bosworth Field, the Stafford family had another chance of regaining its lost position. Henry Stafford's

---

[1] Encyclopaedia Britannica—Stafford, and Buckingham, Duke of, Stafford.

eldest son, Edward, 3rd Duke of Buckingham, was 'restored in lands, blood and title by Henry VII'. In his position as Constable of England he was very powerful, and when Henry VII was ill in 1507 he was spoken of as a possible successor. At Cambridge he founded Buckingham College, later called Magdalen College. His fall was due to a quarrel with Wolsey, in Henry VIII's reign. He was accused of treason and beheaded in May 1521. His titles were forfeited, his lands taken from him and held by the Crown. Henry VIII in 1522 granted Buckingham Manor to Lord Marney. The name, Buckingham Manor is not used after this date, but is replaced by Buckingham borough. The borough passed to Lord Marney's son, then as there was no heir, back to the Crown and in 1526 to William Carey, whose son sold the borough to Bernard Brocas in 1552[2].

Martyrs in Buckingham

During this period religious changes had been taking place which affected everyone in the country. The ideas of John Wycliffe had lived on after his death in 1384. His followers, the Lollards, worked and preached for a clergy who would return to a simple life of poverty and devotion, and a bible that could be read in English, so that all could understand its message. To the government of the day this was heresy; the Lollards had to be suppressed, and until the Reformation, successive kings had them arrested. When Henry IV came to the throne, the church obtained legal right to the capital punishment of heretics, especially by an Act of 1401, 'De Heretico Comburendo', permitting the burning alive of heretics. This law was enforced vigorously. Lollards who were brought before ecclesiastical courts generally recanted rather than burn, but some preferred to be martyrs, among them some people of Buckingham.

In the Rev. Henry Southwell's *New Book of Martyrs* he gives accounts of these martyrs of Buckingham. Referring to 1506, he says on page 249:—'This year also, one Father Roberts, a priest was convicted of being a Lollard before the Bishop of Lincoln, and burnt alive at Buckingham; he suffered with great constancy, piety and resignation; embraced the faggots, and rejoiced God had accounted him worthy to die for the truth of the gospel'.

The Rev. Roundell says in his lecture of 1857, that in the same year that the priest was burnt, a miller of Missenden was burnt at Buckingham and twenty persons branded on the cheek.

On page 251 of Southwell's book we read that in 1519 . ' . . one Robert Celin, a plain honest man, was condemned by the Bishop of Lincoln and burned alive at Buckingham, for speaking against image worship and pilgrimages'.

[2] V.C.H. Bucks III, page 481.

These burnings would probably take place in the Bull Ring, the smoke would drift over the town, and everyone would smell it. The fire would provide an entertainment for some and a warning for others. The Bull Ring at other times would be used for markets, fairs, for pelting people who were in the stocks and for the baiting of bulls by dogs, all considered to be good fun in medieval times.

The Dissolution of the Monasteries

When Henry VIII came to the throne he inherited the wealth and strong system of government that his father had established. He did not wish England to return to the state of civil war that had existed before his father's reign. He needed a son to succeed him, and his middle-aged wife, Catherine of Aragon had given him a daughter, and no other children. Henry was determined to marry Anne Boleyn, his wife's pretty lady-in-waiting, but he needed to get rid of Catherine first. This would be difficult as divorce was not allowed by the church. Henry convinced himself that he had never been married to Catherine, as he had needed a special ' dispensation ' from the Pope to marry her in the first place. He asked Pope Clement VII to declare that the dispensation had not been valid, but Clement delayed answering; Wolsey fell from favour for failing to obtain the annulment, and the situation was saved by Thomas Cranmer who was made Archbishop of Canterbury and declared at a Church court that Catherine had never been lawfully married to Henry. The way was open for Henry to marry Anne, who soon had a daughter, Elizabeth.

The quarrel with the Pope increased in venom, the Pope declaring that Anne's child was illegitimate, and Henry's parliament passing Acts limiting Papal power and defying his authority. Neither would give way, and in 1535 parliament passed an Act of Supremacy stating that the King and not the Pope was head of the church in England. The way was now open for Henry to reform the church in England.

Some of the monasteries, especially the smaller ones, were badly managed and needed reforming; Thomas Cromwell, who now had the king's ear, produced reports which supported this, though some reports may have been biased. Henry and Cromwell were given the excuse they wanted, the excuse to close the houses and add the wealth of the church to the king's coffers. In 1536 the houses with an annual income of less than £200 were dissolved. In 1538-9 the greater monasteries were dissolved, and property worth about £140,000 a year, almost half the church's annual income, was taken over by the king. Thousands of people were made homeless, and thousands of acres of land were at the disposal of the king, to give away or sell as he chose. Many men bought lands, and supported Henry in his break with Rome, as all their lands would be returned to the church if the Pope was once more recognised as head of the church in England.

Henry's break with Rome had other effects. In 1538 he ordered that the bible in English should be kept and read in every parish church in the country. The burning of Lollards should cease, as the king himself encouraged the use of the English bible. However this was not so. On page 259 Southwell tells us of a man who was cast into prison in Newgate by Bishop Bonner, ' for no other crime than that of reading Tindal's New Testament in St. Paul's Church, London '. This man was chained to a post, by the neck for several days, and died. ' This young man even as the law stood, was not guilty of any offence, the king having granted a license to every person to read the bible; but Bonner did not consult the king, and as for Lord Cromwell he was dead, and for a short time all hope of a reformation forsook England '.

Buckingham was the scene of another martyrdom at this time, as Southwell writes on the same page, ' Dreadful persecutions were at this time carried on at Lincoln under Dr. Langland, the Bishop of that diocese—at Buckingham Thomas Bainard and James Moreton, the one for reading the Lord's Prayer in English, the other for reading St. James' Epistle, were both condemned and burned alive '.

Buckingham at the time of the Dissolution

The Dissolution affected Buckingham as it did other places. The prebendary at that time was Richard Pate (prebendary from 1528-1542), and this prebend was the second most valuable in the kingdon. Prebend End Manor, which included Gawcott Manor, was taken from the church and in 1547 Edward VI granted it to Edward, Duke of Somerset, who held it through Queen Mary's reign[3]. As holder of the prebendal estate the Duke of Somerset held the advowson of the church of Buckingham, which passed on with the estate to the Denton and Coke families at a later date.

From 10th April, 1538 to 12th January, 1561, Robert Hall was vicar at Buckingham. These would be difficult times for him, as he took over his duties when religious houses were being closed throughout the country. He may have lost his home, as the Manor House, which was part of the Prebend End Manor was taken from the church about this time. The twisted chimney was probably added about 1520 when Will Smith was the prebendary and Thomas Cause the vicar. Robert Hall may have been without a house for a while as the present vicarage was not yet built.

Although many monasteries had been abolished by Henry VIII, the small chantries remained where priests held daily services. These were dealt with in Edward VI's reign, much of the money going to the Duke of Northumberland and his friends. Matthew Stratton's chantry was said at the time of the Dissolution to be dedicated to St. John the Baptist and St. Thomas a Becket. Its

[3] V.C.H. Bucks III, page 483.

34

annual income was 69s. 4d. and its ornaments were worth 48s. 4d. In 1540 John Josslyn, the king's servant was granted three tenements in Buckingham, which were part of the property of the chantry, and in 1553 a grant of the chapel with its appurtenances was made to Thomas Reeve and Giles Isham. Further grants of land and tenements were made in 1568 to Sir Thomas Newnham and in 1590 to William Tipper and Thomas Dawe[4]. The Victoria History says that the building was later used for the Latin School founded here in the 16th century. Roundell (page 5) thought that the Chantry Chapel was suppressed in 1546 with its revenues worth £5 6s. 4d.

Browne Willis (page 81) says that ' Dame Isobel Denton . . . . gave by her Will about the year 1540, four marks yearly to a priest to teach Children in this Town, in Augmentation of his Living for twenty Years; of which eight years were then said to have expired, Anno 2 Edward VI '.

' Which Prince, in order to found the Said School, as I have been informed, gave a Stipend of £10 8s. 0¾d. per Annum, payable out of the Exchequer, on taking away the lands of St. Thomas Acon's College in London, which lay near this place: And so the Chantry Chapel of St. John the Baptist in this Borough . . . having been obtained from the Proprietors thereof, became converted into a School and hath continued one ever since '.

Another Denton in 1613 held Prebend End Manor, Gawcott and Hillesden, and later in the same century a Denton rebuilt the Master's house attached to the school.

When Edward VI used a small part of the huge royal revenues to found schools, he may have taken over the Isobel Denton bequest and incorporated it in his new school. The school is said to have started in 1552 in Browne Willis's list, the master appointed by Isobel Denton being still in office. He was Henry Webster, afterwards curate of Buckingham, where he died in 1569. The next master was Joseph Williams, then in 1574 Alexander Sheppard taught there, became Vicar of Whitchurch in 1580, but returned to Buckingham in 1599 as vicar. The next master was Thomas Potter, of whom Browne Willis says ' There was, in the year 1599, an Inhibition issued out against him by the Archbishop of Canterbury, John Whitgift, that he should not preach nor teach School in Villa de Bucks '.

Another master, Richard Earle was discharged by the corporation at Lady Day 1625 for neglect of the school, but later became Vicar of Stowe. The next few masters are mentioned only by name but in 1660 Thomas Stephens was appointed, known among the boys as ' Whipping Tom ', and described by Willis as an excellent schoolmaster who bred up several good scholars.

[4] Browne Willis, pages 48, 81. V.C.H. Bucks III, page 486.

The Old Parish Church of SS Peter and Paul [5]

Sheahan thought that the old parish church, which used to be in what is now the old cemetery, was built in the 13th century. It was a cruciform building with chancel, nave with aisles, two large transepts and a square tower supporting a spire of wood, covered with lead, the height of the spire from the ground being 163 feet. All agreed that it was a handsome building, of which the town could be proud. Archdeacon Ruding, during his time at Buckingham (1471-1481) rebuilt or restored the chancel and added an aisle or transept. He also rebuilt the St. John the Baptist chapel, and gave to the parish church a very valuable manuscript bible, which is now in the parish church on Castle Hill.

Local people helped with the development of the old church. A cross aisle or transept was built by Richard Fowler who in the reign of Edward IV played an important part in the life of Buckingham. Another aisle was built by Fernando Poulton, whose family held Bourton Manor in 1629; this aisle contained the burial place for his family. The south transept, called St. Rumbold's Aisle contained the shrine and chapel of the saint, whose fame was so great that pilgrims flocked to his wells and springs. According to Roundell, one well was at Astrop in the parish of King's Sutton, three at Brackley and several at Buckingham. The principal one at Buckingham, near Bath Lane was excavated by the Archaeological Society. Sutton, Bishop of Lincoln in 1280 forbade the visiting of St. Rumbold's wells within the diocese, as he considered the practice superstitious. But St. Rumbold must have brought a considerable amount of money to Buckingham, and the visiting of the well must have started again, as Sheahan says that so many people came, that an inn or hotel was built for them at the west end of the old church. This Pilgrims Inn was standing towards the end of the 18th century, and would probably have been in Hunter Street.

Richard Fowler helped with the completion of Rumbold's Aisle and the new tomb. In his will he asked ' that there be set a coffyn or a chest, curiously wrought and gilt, as it apperteynith, for to lay in the bones of the same sainte, and that this also to be done, in all things at my cost and charge '.

According to the Victoria History, this chantry to St. Rumbold is first mentioned in 1449, when the vicarage was already instituted. The parishioners were doubtful about the legality of their position, and the king founded a gild in honour of the Holy Trinity, St. Mary and St. Rumbold, with four wardens, with brethren and sisters, having a common seal and power to elect new members, acquire land and to meet and organise their affairs. Permission was given to found a chantry of one chaplain at the altar of St. Rumbold to celebrate divine service ' for the good estate of Henry VI and his

[5] Sheahan, page 235. Browne Willis, page 61.

36

queen and of their own souls'. Lipscomb says on page 583 that this brotherhood or gild in 1549 had an annual value of £17 3d. 7d. with John Temys and William Godfrey as clerks with no other living and two parish clerks each with 13s. 4d. per week and 13s. 4d. to the poor every Good Friday. At the suppression of the chantries, the value given by the Victoria History was £21 7s. 3d. and two priests were supported. The lands of this chantry were granted to William Sawle and William Bridges in 1549 and to two other men in 1550 and 1607. Browne Willis says on page 48, ' 1554, Grant to Peter Temple of a Messuage and Garden in Buckingham and a Messuage called Mean-House there belonging to the Trinity Fraternity'. Peter Temple was associated with Stowe.

Barton's Hospital[6]

At the Suppression, Barton's Chantry and Hospital were valued at £26 7s. 0d. annually, and the ornaments were worth 10s. The six almshouses seem to have been bought by Dorothy Dayrell who died in 1583 and left them to the poor of Buckingham, with an endowment of £5 4s. 0d. to provide the groat apiece to six poor people of the original endowment. The old houses of the original endowment in 1431 were pulled down and rebuilt in 1701, and these were replaced in 1910 by the ones now standing.

Castle House[7]

Castle House was still the most important house in the town. In 1431 it had passed to John Barton junior, and on his death to William Fowler and his heirs. William Fowler held a considerable amount of property in Buckingham; tenements acquired from the Bartons and other people in East Street, West Street, Well Street, and Castle Street, and also 'le Draperie' and 'le Shoprewe'. When he died in 1452 his son Richard succeeded to Barton's property. Richard Fowler was a favourite of Edward IV, the Yorkist king who made him Chancellor of the Duchy of Lancaster. He was also a Knight of the Shire and represented Buckinghamshire in parliament. This is the Richard Fowler who built the cross-aisle or transept in the old church, and in his will directed that St. Rumbold's Aisle should be completed at his expense, with a shrine for the saint. According to the Victoria History (III 484-5) when Richard died in 1477 he bequeathed a life interest in his ' dwelling-place at Bucks ' to his brother Thomas Fowler, and his plate to his son, Richard, who was a minor. In 1485 Richard and his wife Elizabeth gained all rights to the lands also, and no doubt spent a lot of time at Buckingham until his death in 1528, when his property in Buckingham went to his second son, Edward, who held the property till his death in 1540.

[6] V.C.H. Bucks III, page 488.
[7] V.C.H. Bucks III, page 485. Browne Willis, page 51. Harrison, page 75. Lipscomb II, page 569.

Browne Willis on page 51, gives a conflicting story. He says that Edward Fowler inherited Castle House in 1477 and died in 1541—an almost incredibly long time to hold the property. He also says that Edward, ' who being a Gentleman of great Property (as seems to me) entertained and lodged at this Capital House, Catherine, King Henry VIII's first Queen. For as we are told in Grafton's Chronicle p. 1004, ' She being at Buckingham, an Account was sent thither by the King's General, the Earl of Surrey, of his defeating the Scotch Army in Battle at Flodden Field, and slaying their King James IV, on September 9th, 1513; Part of whose Armour he sent her to this Place, for which she returned Thanks to God, and went a Pilgrimage to Walsingham in Norfolk ".

Henry VIII was away in France waging his own war at this time, and Queen Catherine was left to act as regent and cope with the Scots who took the opportunity of invading England. Catherine collected a force which defeated the Scots at Flodden Field. At the old Borough Offices in Buckingham there was a crucifix which is reputed to have belonged to Catherine of Aragon, and said to have been left by her as a present when leaving the town.

Stowe

Just before the Dissolution the Giffards had acquired from the abbots of Biddlesden and Oseney, a 99 year lease of two properties at Stowe. These were valued at £36 8s. 0d. per year, and were rented to Peter Temple at £82 a year. This Peter Temple was a rising man with an estate at Burton Dassett. He had travelled widely in the midlands for some years, collecting rents and buying and selling properties, many of which came on the market, as church lands were broken up. He had bought two houses in Buckingham in 1554, and by 1571 and 1572 he saw his chance of some land at Stowe.

The Town of Buckingham

During the Wars of the Roses, until 1485, England was unsettled, and the economy suffered. When Henry VII came to the throne he realised that his power depended on, among other things, his wealth, and the wealth of the country. His first parliament, which lasted only from November to December 1485, passed an Act of Resumption which allowed the king to regain possession of all lands which had been sold since 1455, during the Wars of the Roses. This Act was applied vigorously, so that during his first year as king he received a clear profit of £13,633 from his estates, compared with the last year of Edward IV's reign, when only £6,471 had been collected. By tightening up the collection of money from various sources he increased his income so that by 1490 he was a lender rather then a borrower.

In Henry VII's reign the export of woollen cloth increased,

as the continent was supplied by us through Antwerp. Many people benefited from this; the king's revenue increased, the merchants prospered, as did the landowners with flocks of sheep, and the towns where wool was sold and woven into cloth. But at this time Buckingham was suffering a decline in trade which had started even earlier.

The Victoria History[8] gives a picture of the town in 1473, derived from an account of the profits of the borough for that year. There was then a Castle Street, Well Street, and an East Street, which might have been our present Bridge Street. The Draper's Hall in the market-place sounds an imposing building with ' seven bays ' which were rented to traders, but three-quarters of only one of these was let to three people paying 2s. 6d. each. In the square there were twelve shops or sheds and two places for the sale of fish, but eighteen of the stalls were vacant. There was ' le Comyn Bakehouse ' and in Castle Street ' le Corner House ', which cannot be the house in West Street now known by that name. A tavern was opposite the St. John the Baptist Chapel, and William Fowler had a smithy.

Buckingham was still the county town, and in 1496 had the custody of the standard weights and measures for the shire[9]. They were in the custody of the bailiff, and were made from a pattern which was sent from London. In 1509 a bushel, a gallon and a yard of brass which had been used for Buckingham were returned to Westminster, and in 1549 the newly-elected bailiff had delivered to him ' a brasyn Stryke, a brasyn Gallon, a brasyn yard brokyn '.

The town was visited by King Henry VIII[10] on August 28th, 1540. He came with his Privy Council, and stayed long enough for letters to be despatched from here to the Warden of the Fleet, the Sheriffs of London, the Lord Chancellor, the Duke of Norfolk and others.

The assizes were removed from Buckingham to Aylesbury in Henry VIII's reign, through the influence of Chief Justice Baldwin, and the county gaol was also moved there. Browne Willis produces evidence of a gaol still existing in Buckingham; on page 49 of his *Antiquities of Buckingham* he tells of an ancestor of the Earl of Pomfret, called Richard Fermour, who had his estate seized and taken away from him, ' . . . . by relieving one Nicholas Thane, an obnoxious Popish priest, who had been committed a close Prisoner to the Gaol in the Town of Buckingham '. Browne Willis thought that the castle in Buckingham had been used as the ' Ancient Place of Committment of Malefactors within this Shire ', and names many towns where the castles had been used in this way, Cambridge, Chester, Gloucester and through a list alphabetically to York.

[8] V.C.H. Bucks III, page 471.
[9] V.C.H. Bucks III, page 480.
[10] Royal Visits to the Borough of Buckingham, by D. J. Elliott.

Members of Parliament for Buckingham[11]

In 1529 John Haselwood and Edward Sool were elected Members of Parliament for Buckingham. From that date, regular elections were held, and it seems that the bailiff and burgesses were the electorate. By this time people were more eager than formerly to serve in parliament, and the local gentry were willing to represent the town.

Lipscomb (page 560-561) gives a list of the M.P.'s from 1545 to 1841. Some surnames appear frequently, and are those belonging to the families who owned estates nearby. The Giffard family are the first on the list. Henry Cary was a member in 1547 when he held Buckingham Manor, and in 1554 and 1555; his surname also occurs later. The Verneys of Claydon House served from 1623 to Victorian times, when this list ends. The Dentons who bought Prebend End Manor in 1613 are strongly represented from 1603 to 1772. Francis Ingoldsby of Lenborough was member in the Rump Parliament. The Temple family dominates the list from 1639, the Grenvilles appear in 1734 and the Nugents in 1784, the members being entirely from this family for many years.

Empty Shops at Buckingham

Buckingham still held fairs and markets, but they cannot have been so well attended as in former times. From being a prosperous place in Edward III's reign, when in 1337 representatives had been sent to a trade council, by 1473 only twelve of the thirty stalls in the market were in use. By 1540 the town was in such a bad state that it was included with thirty-five other towns in a list of towns with decayed houses. The Act concerning this list, directed the owners of ' these waste lands to build upon them sufficient and suitable houses, within the space of three years, next after passing of this Act '. If they failed to obey, the land would be taken from them and given to the lord of the manor, or to ' the owner of any rent charge upon it ', or to the Corporation of the Borough, provided that one of them will build on the land[12].

The earlier writers have blamed the economic decline of the town on the removal of the Wool Staple to Calais. It was thought that Buckingham, like York, Lincoln, Bristol and Winchester had been a Staple Town, but according to Roundell this was not so. Buckingham had its own Wool Hall or Drapers Hall and was a local centre for trading in wool, but a staple was not fixed here. While sheep and therefore wool was being grown in the neighbourhood, Buckingham should have continued as a small, local collecting point, and the removal of the staple to Calais should not have caused such a marked decline.

The sheep farming on the chalk country to the north would

[11] V.C.H. Bucks III, page 478. Browne Willis, page 41. Sheahan, page 228.
[12] Roundell, page 11.

involve enclosure of lands; the change from corn growing which took much labour, to sheep which needed only a man and a dog to watch them, would cause unemployment. Less money would circulate in Buckingham and the stalls would close.

In 1455, in the first fighting of the Wars of the Roses, Humphrey Stafford was killed. In 1460 at Northampton, his father Humphrey Stafford, Duke of Buckingham was killed, leaving the town without a protector during the fighting of the following years. The Stafford family suffered a greater blow when Henry Stafford was beheaded in 1483 for treason, and his son shared the same fate in 1521. The town may have suffered economically for the attainder of its most important citizens, and this would add to its troubles.

The Queen Mary Charter[13]

In 1130 London and Lincoln offered Henry I money to free themselves from the control of the officers of the shire, and to be allowed to pay their dues directly to the Exchequer. London offered 100 marks of silver ' that they might have a sheriff of their own choice ', and Lincoln offered 4 marks in gold ' that they might hold their city of the king in chief '. The two cities were granted their charters. By 1189, the end of Henry II's reign, only five boroughs apart from London were directly responsible to the Crown for their dues, and their privileges might be taken away at any time. When Richard I needed money for the crusades he bargained with towns for their charters. Any town which could afford it bought a charter to exclude the shire officers and to give themselves more independence. King John also sold charters and no doubt Buckingham had as much chance as any town to buy its independence, the only snag being the money.

Other advantages in having a charter were freedom from some tolls, the right to hold fairs and markets (Buckingham already had this right), the right to levy tolls on non-burgesses of the town, and the right for the town to regulate its own trade.

In 1554 Buckingham was granted its first charter of incorporation. Queen Mary granted it at the earnest entreaty of the inhabitants of the borough, in return for their loyalty during the rebellion of the Duke of Northumberland. During the rebellion Queen Mary had fled to Framlingham Castle, but she was proclaimed as Queen in Buckinghamshire, then was escorted to London by 1,000 men from Buckinghamshire, Northamptonshire and Oxfordshire. Aylesbury, Buckingham and other towns in the county received charters in thanks.

The Victoria History states that as early as the 14th century there is a record of a bailiff of Buckingham, but this is doubtful[14]. The bailiff was chief officer of the borough, and had some respons-

---

[13] Browne Willis, page 86. Lipscomb II, page 561. V.C.H. Bucks III, pages 476-480.
[14] V.C.H. Bucks III, page 477.

ibility in law enforcement. Writs were directed to him, he presided over the portmote or borough court, and he was responsible to the lord of the borough for profits arising from the overlordship. In the Domesday Survey Buckingham had twenty-six burgesses, while in 1549 there were nineteen names in a list of burgesses, including three widows of former burgesses.

The charter made the town a Free Borough corporate, and the bailiff and twelve burgesses one Body corporate. The property qualification for the chief burgesses was that they should have property bringing an annual income of 13s. 4d. or have goods with a total value of £20, meaning that they were propertied men but not necessarily big landowners. The charter named the first bailiff, John Lambert, and the first burgesses, who together. would form the Common Council of the Borough. Edward Chamberlain was appointed the first Steward. His duties were to act as a justice of the peace, and to share with the bailiff the presidency of the borough Court of Record. The new stewards were to be elected by the bailiff and burgesses. The burgesses were elected for life, and when one died, the bailiff and remaining burgesses elected another, from the 'inhabitants' of the borough.

The bailiff was appointed for a year, from the day of his election, which was the feast of St. Philip and St. James. The chief burgesses nominated two of their members, and the remaining inhabitants elected one as bailiff for the following year. He presided over a court held every three weeks, together with the steward and three principal burgesses. This court which tried cases relating to debts, contracts, and other actions not exceeding £5, was not used much and ceased in 1818. Two Court Leets[15], petty criminal courts for the punishment of small offences, could be held yearly, and two views of frankpledge, where a man not in a household of some importance, should prove that he was part of a frankpledge, a group of twelve people who were mutually responsible for the production of one of them in court. For the privilege of holding these courts the borough paid £1 annually to the Exchequer. The bailiff was also the Escheator, Coroner, ' for us, Our Heirs, and Successors, and the Clerk of Our Market of Us, Our Heirs, and Successors, within the Borough aforesaid '.

The bailiff and burgesses had the right to elect two members of parliament; the small size of the electorate later gave rise to a great deal of corruption. The borough was given a seal, with the right to break and replace it whenever the corporation wished. There are now two seals of Buckingham, an old one of silver and a more recent brass one. A market was allowed every Tuesday, and two fairs per year, 'together with the Beast-Market to continue during the Time of those Fairs '.

15 V.C.H. Bucks III, page 478.

The bounds of the parish were fixed, the borough was allowed ' one Prison or Gaol in some convenient Place within the Borough aforesaid ', an assize, measure of weight for bread, wine, beer and ' other Victuals, and also a Measure and Weight for all Things, for the Amendment, Punishment, and Correction of them so often as it shall be needful and expedient '. The borough could make its own bye-laws, so long as they did not conflict with the laws of the kingdom.

The rights of jurisdiction which had previously been held by the lord of the manor were now held by the corporation, which had the authority to arrange many town affairs as it wished. Now Buckingham was independent and could go ahead.

CHAPTER IV

A CHARTERED BOROUGH 1554–1642

WHEN Queen Mary came to the throne, Englishmen once more had to think carefully about their religion if they wished to live. Mary was the devoted daughter of Catherine of Aragon, and had been brought up as a Catholic. Her faith had persisted through the divorce of her mother and her own banishment from court to Hatfield to act as lady-in-waiting to her young sister Elizabeth. After Anne Boleyn's death she made an act of submission to her father, and was eventually restored to her place in succession to the throne, but she was still forced to acknowledge herself illegitimate.

Throughout her father's and brother Edward's reigns she held to her religion, and when her turn came to rule, she determined to restore Catholicism and papal authority to England. Her first parliament annulled her mother's divorce and repealed her brother's religious legislation, and other parliaments reluctantly repealed Henry's anti-papal laws and allowed England to be under papal authority: but holders of lands formerly belonging to the church were allowed to keep them. Heretics once again could be burnt, but fortunately none were burnt at Buckingham.

Robert Hall was vicar of Buckingham from 1538 to 1561, so had to adapt himself to Henry's break with Rome, then to Mary's return of papal supremacy. When Elizabeth came to the throne there was a change again. Elizabeth, who had been brought up as a Protestant, restored the Act of Supremacy, making herself head of the church. Some bishops disagreed and were replaced, and the country settled down to relative religious toleration, and a time of increased trade at home and abroad.

In 1565, eleven years after obtaining a charter of incorporation, the town arms were ratified[1]. Browne Willis reports an entry in the Visitation Book in the Herald Office in London, by William Harvey, Clarencieux King of Arms. The arms are described as ' Per Pale Gules and Sable, a Swan chained, gorged with a Ducal Coronet, his Wings expanded '. At the time of the Visitation to Buckingham, the bailiff and burgesses were present, also ' John Hokeley Town Clerk and William White Under Bailiff '. It is interesting that a town clerk is mentioned, as he is not included in the Mary Charter; but in 1835 was appointed by the steward and acted as his deputy[2].

Henry Gough writing about 1867 in the Records of Buckinghamshire Volume III, page 249, gives an account of the way in which the swan may have come to be associated with Buckingham. He

[1] Browne Willis page 106.
[2] V.C.H. Bucks III, page 478.

thought that the swan may have been the device of Sweyn, King of Denmark. After the Norman Conquest, a powerful chief, Suene, of Rayleigh in Essex, joined the invaders and was confirmed in the possession of his lands as a reward, and was then known as Swene of Essex. He is thought to have been of Danish descent, and may have had the swan as his device, as the Bourchiers, who were descended from him had the swan as a crest, and were not entitled to it otherwise.

A part of the Essex lands was later obtained by the Mandeville family, who probably had the swan as their badge, obtaining it along with the lands. When the last William de Mandeville died, the great estates known as the Honour of Essex, went by marriage to the Bohun family. A white swan, usually with closed wings, was frequently used as a ' family badge ' of the Bohuns, on seals and even on ' an entire bed of green, powdered with white swans ' which was bequeathed by one Bohun to his son in 1319. At this time the swan's wings were usually closed, but sometimes open, apparently depending on the whim of the earl or the artist.

The Bohun family ended with two heiresses, both of whom made brilliant marriages, and both of whose husbands had the white swan as their badge. These husbands may have added the golden coronet and chain. Mary de Bohun married Henry of Lancaster who later became Henry IV. He, like Henry V, used the white swan as part of his badge, gorged and chained and with wings sometimes expanded and at other times closed. The other Bohun sister, Alianor or Eleanor, married Thomas of Woodstock, the youngest son of Edward III, who in 1376 was appointed to the Bohun office of Constable of England, and the next year, at the coronation of Richard II was created Earl of Buckingham. This was the first time that the swan as a badge, was associated with Buckingham. The seals of Duchess Eleanor and her husband show swans in varied positions, with wings expanded and closed, gorged with coronets. The sepulchral brass of the Duchess Eleanor in the Chapel of St. Edmund at Westminster was decorated with swans generally with wings closed, sometimes gorged and chained, and sometimes not.

Anne, daughter of Eleanor and Thomas of Woodstock, married into the Stafford family, and her son Humphrey, sixth Earl of Stafford, was created Duke of Buckingham in 1444. He was killed in the battle of Northampton in 1460; Henry, the second Duke was beheaded at Salisbury in 1483, and Edward, the third and last Duke was beheaded on Tower Hill in 1521, when the family lost their ducal rank, their hereditary office of Lord High Constable of England, which had been confirmed to them as representatives of the Bohuns.

Examples of the Bohun swan being used by the Staffords include the Garter stall-plate of Humphrey Stafford who was elected a companion of the Order in 1429; this is illustrated opposite page

261 in Mr. Gough's article. It is probable that during the time that the Stafford family bore the title of Duke of Buckingham, the swan became associated with the town and shire. Boutell's ' Heraldry ', Plate XII, opposite page 165, shows the Stafford knot on a parted field of black and red. The livery colours of the Staffords, black and red, sable and gules, form the parted field on which the town and county swans are represented, indicating that they were adopted about this time. The reference by Drayton to the men of Buckingham in 1415 ' Under the swan, the arms of that old town ', may be premature, but by 1566, at the Visitation by William Harvey, Clarencieux King of Arms, the town arms were sufficiently established for him to write ' These are the arms antiently belonging to the town and borough of Buckingham '. Later a chain was usually added, crossing the swan's back, as is seen in Speed's map of 1610. This chain does not, however appear in the shield over the tower entrance of the parish church, which was finished in 1781. The Buckingham swan now has expanded wings and is gorged and chained.

1568 was a memorable year for Buckingham. The charter and the town arms had added to its importance, and in 1568 it was honoured by two visits. On the 24th of June the Archbishop of Canterbury issued a commission to Thomas Godwyn, Dean of Canterbury, and Thomas Cowper, Dean of Christ Church, Oxford, ordering them to come to Buckingham and hold a Visitation there[3], so that all ecclesiastical matters could be seen to, as at that time there was no bishop of Lincoln. It must have caused a great commotion, when such important men came, but it would be nothing compared with the excitement on the 25th of August when Queen Elizabeth and her train of followers passed through Buckingham. An account of the visit is on folio 380 of the Borough Records, Roundell's rather shortened version reads, " On the 25th day of August, 1568, the high and mighty Princess, Queen Elizabeth, came in progresse to the Burrow of Buckingham in the County of Bucks, and at the utmost part of the limits of the liberties of the said Burrow, on the North part of the same, in the way named Towcester way, the Bayliff, and the twelve principal Burgesses of the said Burrow, made their most humble submission and received her Grace. Whereupon Her Highness did admit the said Bayliff to be her chamberlain within the said Burrow by delivering him one white wand. And to pay proper honour to the said Burrow, Her Majesty had, in a most triumphant manner, her sword Royall and maces borne, and trumpets blowne, until she came to the mansion house of the Rector or Prebendary of the said Burrow, when her Highness rested dinner time, and after dinner ended, Her Grace proceeded forward to the town of Bicester, in the County of Oxford, the said Bayliff attending her person from the said parsonage house, until at a certain bridge, called Dudley Bridge, which leads to Tingewick, in

[3] Roundell page 12.

46

the said county of Bucks, and there John Bauldwine, Esq., being Sheriff of the County, expecting Her Grace's coming executed his office as before ".

According to Lipscomb's list, there was no prebendary of Buckingham at this time, as Richard Cox had surrendered his prebend in 1547 when the Prebend End Manor had been granted to Edward, Duke of Somerset. From the entry in the Borough Records, it seems that the rector or vicar, was still living in what was then Prebend End manor house, and is now the Manor House.

In Henry VIII's reign the assizes had been removed to Aylesbury by Justice Baldwin, and this was confirmed by an Act passed in 1572 for " Keeping the Assizes at Aylesbury "[4]. The assizes were held at Aylesbury for some years, but towards the end of the next century, Thomas Baskerville reported that the assizes were at Buckingham. The movement of the administrative and judicial centre to Aylesbury took some centuries, and in the meantime the county had two centres—Aylesbury and Buckingham, with Wycombe as a lesser centre.

In 1574 the Queen granted to Edward Grimston sen., and Edward Grimston jun., " the Castle Farm in Buckingham, and two mills, called Castle Mills, with four acres of meadow, called Milne House, and Buckingham River with twenty messuages and cottages adjoining, late parcel of the lands of Edward, late Duke of Buckingham attainted "[5]. The Duke was Edward Stafford, enemy of Wolsey, and Lipscomb thought that part of the property was the remains of the castle, reduced to the condition of a farmhouse.

In the same year, Bernard Brocas, who had inherited the lordship of Buckingham borough in 1557, passed his rights in the borough to the corporation. In 1572 he had leased tenements in Castle Street, Well Street, and other places, to William Brooke, glover, Adam Costardyne and others, who were apparently burgesses, at a nominal rent for 2000 years. The corporation paid a quit-rent of 40s. a year to the representatives of Bernard Brocas, and this was later bought by the Temple family of Stowe, and was paid to the Dukes of Buckingham and Chandos. This quit-rent was no longer paid in 1909 when Harrison wrote his book[6]. Browne Willis and Sheahan say that Brocas passed to the corporation " this Manor of Buckingham together with the tolls, etc. of the Markets and Fairs ". As Mary's Charter already gave to the corporation the profits from markets and fairs, this later right appears to be nominal, but would be acquired by the corporation to make sure that it held all manorial rights.

[4] V.C.H. Bucks IV, page 528.
[5] Lipscomb II, pages 570, 571.
[6] V.C.H. Bucks III, page 481.   Browne Willis page 28.

Christ's Hospital[7]

Queen Elizabeth founded Christ's Hospital by charter in 1598, to provide refuge for 36 maimed soldiers dwelling in Buckingham or the three hundreds. It is said to have been erected on the site of the St. Laurence hospital for lepers which had apparently closed in the 14th century, probably as a result of the reduction of the economy after the Black Death. Nearly all the hospitals of the county came to an end at that period. In 1666 Christ's Hospital sheltered " seven antient women ", and the endowment included the hospital house, a yard and orchard, probably leading down to the river, and nearby a wool-market, and wool fair. In 1836 the garden was let for £5 a year, the piece of ground formerly called the Wool-Hall was let to the Duke of Buckingham for £11 a year.

The Duke later built Butchers' Shambles there, and it is now Barclays Bank. The hospital also received £1 a year in rent for the Fleece, a house near Butchers' Row, which had been bequeathed in 1598 by Robert Harris, and £5 a year from the corporation out of the profits of two fairs.

The old buildings became dilapidated and were rebuilt in 1897 for £843 7s. 9d., the money coming from sale of the garden at the back of the hospital, sale of the land left for charities by Katherine Agard and Dorothy Dayrell in 1574, and some money left by James Harrison and others.

Castle House[8]

Catherine of Aragon had been entertained at Castle House in 1513; Catherine's daughter Mary had granted the town a charter in 1554, when Edward Fowler's son, Gabriel owned the Barton house and property. When Gabriel died in 1582 he left the estate to his son Richard Fowler, with instructions that on coming of age he should sell the Buckingham property, described as a farm in the tenure of Raphael More. In 1590-1591 Richard sold the estate, " a messuage and six acres of pasture ", to Francis and Edward Dayrell, who about three months later transferred it to John Lambert or Lambard. John Lambert enjoyed his house for only a short time, as in 1597-1598 Theophilus Adams claimed the estate. Mr. Adams had been granted Barton's chantry in 1585, and in 1597 claimed Barton's property under a Crown grant, as lands given to superstitious uses. In accordance with John Barton's will, money from the property had been used to support a priest who served in the chantry; Harrison says that £6 13s. 4d. per annum had been charged on the property. Adams won his case and obtained a grant of the land, but in 1607 John Lambert negotiated an agreement and bought out Adams' claim. When John died

---

[7] V.C.H. Bucks III, pages 486, 488. Sheahan pages 240, 246. Harrison page 34. Roundell page 39. Browne Willis page 84. V.C.H. Bucks I, page 392.

[8] V.C.H. Bucks III, pages 485, 488. Browne Willis pages 51-53. Lipscomb II, page 569. Harrison page 76.

in 1611, his son William inherited the house, and with his wife Mary, made considerable alterations to it. They erected the elaborately carved mantel over the fireplace in what is now the council chamber, and left dates from 1617 to 1624 in other parts of the house. They also made an innovation by bringing piped water to the house, from one of St. Rumbold's wells. The water was brought in pipes which were marked ' W & ML Anno 1619 ', and according to Harrison, a conduit house was built over the well.

When William died in 1626 his son John, still a minor inherited the estate, which by then included two water mills and an orchard near Podds Lane, now called Moreton Road. He died in 1632 while still a minor, the property passing to his fourteen year old sister, May.

The Manors of Buckingham[9]

The rights of Buckingham Manor had been passed to the corporation by Bernard Brocas in 1574. Until 1560 Bourton Manor had followed the same descent as Buckingham Manor, but from that date their paths parted. In 1560 Bernard Brocas sold Bourton Manor to Nicholas West, his wife and his son, and the manor stayed in this family until some time before 1629. Meadowland called Goosemead, part of Bourton Manor, was bought by Ferdinand Poulton before this date, to add to the estate that he already owned in Bourton. The whole of the manor was later acquired by Ferdinand's son Francis.

Of the two Lenborough manors, one had been held, in Norman days, by Walter Giffard, the overlordship following the same descent as that of Buckingham and Bourton Manors. The land, as opposed to the overlordship, passed to the Inglefield family in the 13th century, and was leased by them to the de Langetots for many years. After 1346 no more is heard of the de Langetots, but the Inglefields held the knight's fee which represented the manor in 1460. By 1493 the manor had passed to Ralph Ingoldsby, whose family still held it in 1613. The park at Lenborough was enclosed in 1617 by Sir Richard Ingoldsby who held the manor at that time.

The other Lenborough Manor had been held by Odo, Bishop of Bayeux, then had been granted to Reading Abbey until the Dissolution. Some time before 1636 the Ingoldsbys absorbed this manor with the other land they held at Lenborough.

Prebend End Manor of Buckingham with Gawcott had been granted, for his lifetime, to Edward, Duke of Somerset in 1547, to Henry Seymour in 1569 and 1595 for himself and two other men. By 1609 it was again in the possession of the Crown. The same year it was granted permanently to Sir Robert Brett, who sold it in 1613 to Sir Thomas Denton, whose family played a big part in the history of the district.

[9] V.C.H. Bucks III, pages 480-486.

Before the Civil War

When James I became King of England on Elizabeth's death, he had already been King of Scotland for many years, and he told parliament that he was an old and experienced king. Nevertheless, he found the complexities of English economics more than he could cope with. His main energies and best years had been spent in obtaining the throne of England, and when he achieved his ambition, he found that parliament had to agree to any taxation, and an English parliament was difficult to control. Sir Thomas Denton and Sir Edward Terrel were the members of parliament for Buckingham in 1603, Sir Edward Terrel dying and being replaced by Sir Francis Goodwin. In the brief ' Addled Parliament ' of 1614 Sir Thomas Denton once again represented Buckingham, this time partnered by Thomas Teringham. In his efforts to obtain the money which parliament would not grant, James tried other methods, including the sale of monopolies, one of which may have affected Buckingham. This was William Cockayne's project in 1614, to pay the king £300,000 a year for a monopoly for exporting finished cloth, and the prohibition of the export of it unfinished. This nearly ruined the cloth trade, as exports slumped, clothworkers became unemployed and the Dutch and Flemings began to make their own cloth. It was abandoned in 1617, but Buckingham may have been affected during that time.

In 1610 John Speed produced a series of maps of some of the English counties. In one corner of the one of Buckinghamshire is a plan of Buckingham, the county town. This map shows not only the arrangement of the streets, but also the extent of the town. The town looked then very similar to today, as its arrangment is dependent on the curves of the river; the centre is much the same, but the town has grown around the outskirts. Castle Street had houses on both sides of the road, but led to a Castle Hill different from today, as it was open ground with a few small houses and the ruins of a castle, as described by Thomas Baskerville towards the end of the century[10], " The town is pretty large, with good inns, and surrounds a green mound on which remains some ruins of a castle. There is no town hall for the judges to sit in for the assizes, and so sheds are erected for the purpose against the ruinous castle walls ". The assizes apparently had returned to the town at this time.

There were a few houses on Well Street; and Water Lane, now called Bridge Street led to the river but not to a bridge. The bridge for the road to London, called " Sherifes Bridge ", or later, Woolpack Bridge, was described by Samuel Pepys who visited the town on 8th June, 1668, as "A fair bridge here with many arches",[10] and was in the position of the present Iron Bridge at Ford Street.

The parish church is shown in the old churchyard, with a Prebend House at the south-east corner, in a different position from the

[10] V.C.H. Bucks III, page 472.

Manor House, which was then standing, and different from the present Prebend House in Hunter Street. Roundell says that the Pilgrim's Inn was standing in 1610, and would probably be in Hunter Street. Houses extended down Mill Lane and the other side of Lords Bridge a little way along the Gawcott Road, Lenborough Road and Mount Pleasant. This district was then called " Prebend Ende beyond the Water ". West Street was well built up, with houses extending to the Corner House, which was probably then a busy bell-foundry[11], started by the Apowells some time before 1552, when John Appowell was involved in a legal action to recover a debt. In 1567 the churchwardens of Thame started paying Appowell for a bell he had cast, and in 1569 they were paying him " for the Cariinge of the bell to Buckingham and bringinge yt home agayne ". John Appowell died in 1577, having been bailiff three times and also churchwarden. John was followed in the business by his son George, who died soon afterwards, and the bell foundry closed for at least five years.

The business seems to have been taken over by Robert Newcombe and Bartholomew Atton who had been trained in the Leicester foundry where Robert's father worked. In 1585-6 the churchwardens of Wing were paying for a bell cast at Buckingham, and a bell at Passenham and one at Hoggeston were also probably cast by these men. " ROBERT NEWCOMBE MADE ME " was on a bell at Hardwick, and Bartholomew Atton's name was on bells at Tingewick, Drayton Parslow, Steeple Claydon, Radclive and other places.

Robert Newcombe died in 1591, and Bartholomew Atton seems to have retired about 1613, and been followed in the business by his son, Robert, who cast bells for Winslow, Grendon Underwood and other places. Robert died in 1628, two years before his father, Bartholomew. After Robert's death a few bells were made with his name on them, but his former assistant, Nathaniel Bolter may have been the founder. The foundry seems to have closed about 1633 but the Atton family continued in Buckingham as drapers.

Across the road from the Corner House is Castle House, which was owned by John Lambert in 1610. In the space in front of Castle House, called the Horse Fair, stood the market cross[12], which is now in the old churchyard. Possibly in those days it was carved and unbroken, but at the end of the 18th century it was moved into the garden of a nearby public house, the Dun Cow, where it was converted into a sun-dial. In 1844 it was taken to Preston Bissett, then later to Lillingstone Lovell, and in 1858 was given to the Rev. W. Perkins of Twyford, who returned it to the town. At first it stood in the vicarage garden but was later placed in the old churchyard, in the position of the western entrance of the old church.

[11] V.C.H. Bucks III, page 472. Harrison page 77.
    The Church Bells of Buckinghamshire by A. H. Cocks, M.A., page 174.
[12] Harrison page 71.

In the centre of the town, the Old Latin School was functioning with James Smith as master. The passage way called The Chewar can be seen in the map, but the Market Square and High Street were more open then than now, with only a few scattered buildings down the centre of the street, and no castellated Old Gaol, which had not yet been built. A Wool Hall was on the site of Barclays Bank, and later the same space was occupied by the Shambles. Christ's Hospital would be in its present position, with the pillory between it and the Wool Hall. There may have been more than one pillory, as later there was one in the Cow Fair.

A house[13] would then be standing on the site of National Westminster Bank. During the demolition of this building, which was previously the Buckingham Trustee Savings Bank and W. H. Deeley, the fishmonger and fruiterer, some wall paintings were found to be more extensive than had been expected. This late fifteenth century house had wall paintings downstairs which covered much of the walls, and included a Tudor coat of arms in many colours on a background of red and yellow stripes, with a portcullis on one side of the coat of arms and a Tudor rose on the other. These symbols were repeated as carvings on the brackets at the ends of a beam across the entrance passage. An ornate frieze at ceiling level contained imaginary beasts and the initials I.L. Upstairs the paintings were largely in black and white, and above the upper ceiling in the attic area were painted scroll patterns in red and yellow on the bare roofing timbers—a feature that had not been suspected. The artists may have been called Russel as this name was included in the designs.

There were no houses up Podds Lane, now Moreton Road, but houses extended to the end of North End Square.

The craftsmen of Buckingham were organised by this time into craft-gilds, with four fellowships or societies[14], namely—

(1) The Mercers, which included ' Mercers, Grocers, Haberdashers, Linendrapers, Woollendrapers, Clothiers, Silkmen, Goldsmiths, Apothecaries, Salters, Ironmongers, Chandlers (honey or wax), and Hat or Capmakers '.

(2) The Cordwainers, which included ' Shoemakers, Tanners, Glovers, Parchmentmakers, Saddlers, Collarmakers, Girdlemakers, Poynters, and Poyntmakers '.

(3) The Tailors, which included ' Taylors, Dyers, Fullers, Weavers, Smiths, Glaziers, Pewterers, Brasiers, Fletchers, Furbishers and Painters '

(4) The Butchers, which included ' Butchers, Bakers, Brewers, Cooks and Millers '.

The Buckingham gilds evidently included in their membership all or most of the trades in the borough, and the town seems to

[13] Buckinghamshire County Museum Report, April 1966-March 1968.
    Photographs of house belonging to Buckingham Archaeological Society.
[14] V.C.H. Bucks III, page 479.

Steam Road Locomotive made in Buckingham—1860

The Interior of the Parish Church Buckingham before the addition of the
Chancel in 1865

have been a busy place. The trades include many who had shops to sell goods, and also people who made the goods. The textile trades are well represented as might be expected with Buckingham's connection with wool. The gilds served to control the standard of workmanship and also to fine or tax outsiders who traded within the borough. In 1573 these points were included in ordinances drawn up by the bailiff and burgesses by which two of the ' most discretest ' men were to be chosen by the craftsmen as wardens of the gilds, to take their oaths before the bailiff and burgesses and serve for a year in controlling the gilds, and taking those who broke the regulations to the borough court.

A gallon of good wine to the bailiff and burgesses and no more, was paid by a freeman, or the son of a freeman when he wished to enter a gild, but an outsider or ' foreigner ' paid much more. To ' sett open ' their shop windows for selling goods a foreigner paid £4 10s. 0d. if a shoemaker or glover, £3 if a tanner, 40s. if a parch-mentmaker or saddler and 30s. if a girdlemaker, collar-maker or bottle-maker. In 1663 these fees were altered to £15 for admission to the Mercers, who had 27 members, £9 for the Cordwainers with 28 members and £6 for the Butchers and Tailors who had 33 and 29 members respectively.

The gilds operated a closed shop, keeping out all who had not paid their dues, but they enforced seven year apprenticeship schemes. The rules governing the gilds were repeated in 1690, but there is no further reference to them after this date as the membership of the gild was identical with the freedom of the borough.

A coach service to London was operating by 1637. Harrison quotes Arber's ' English Garner ', Volume I (1637)—" The carriers of Buckingham do lodge at the King's Head, in the Old Change (London); they come on Wednesdays and Thursdays ". The coach for London left Buckingham over the Sheriff's Bridge, stopping at East Claydon and other places with inns on the way to Aylesbury. The through coaches from London to Banbury or Birmingham may have avoided the centre of town, coming over the Sheriff's Bridge, up Elm Street, into Nelson Street, although Elm Street is quite steep. The coaches which were to stop overnight would probably come along Well Street, to the Square, stopping at the town's inns. These included in their time, the White Hart and Cobham Arms, which occupied the whole of the building from Selaire's hairdressing salon to the corner of Morgan's office. This was one of the regular stops for coaches in Lord Cobham's day.

From Buckingham to Virginia[15]

In 1619 the " Company of Adventurers and Planters of the City of London for the First Colony of Virginia " granted to John Woodliff a patent to plant 200 persons in Virginia before the end

---

[15] R.O.B. Volume 17, page 406. Captain John Woodliff by A. Vere Woodman, F.S.A.

of six years. Eleven years before this, he had spent £62 10s. 0d. on buying five shares, each entitling him to 100 acres of land in a plantation at a place called Ensign. The patent was later altered to the name of Sir Thomas Wainman, and arrangements for the enterprise continued.

On 19th August, 1619 " John Woodliff of the town of Buckingham, esquire " chartered at £33 per month " the good ship called the ' Margaret ' of Bristol of the burden of 45 tons or thereabouts " which was to sail for Virginia with the first fair wind and weather after September 15th. On September 4th, Mr. Woodliff made an agreement with the men who were to establish the plantation, and he was nominated Captain and Governor. The district where the Governor would settle would be called Berkeley Hundred, and elaborate arrangements were made as to the division of the profits from the plantation.

The ' Margaret ' sailed from Bristol on 16th September, 1619, just a year before the Mayflower left Plymouth. One of the first instructions that John Woodliff received for the government of Berkeley was " We ordain that the day of our ship's arrival at the place assigned for plantation in the land of Virginia shall be yearly and perpetually kept holy as a day of thanksgiving to Almighty God ". Their Thanksgiving Day may have been the first celebrated in America. The ' Margaret ' reached Virginia after one storm, and on November 30th anchored at Kecketan in a good harbour.

In 1620 John Woodliff received a grant of 530 acres from Sir George Yardley, to add to his own land, and he may have spent too much of his time on his own affairs, as on August 18th, 1620 his commission as Governor was revoked and two other men were together appointed to supervise the affairs of the colony. By about 1621 only nine of the original thirty-four emigrants survived; this high death rate is explained in a letter from a settler, " you will hear many strange reports both of the death of our own people and of others, yet be not discouraged therein for I thank God I never had my health better. I am persuaded that more do die here of the disease of their mind than of their body by having this country's victuals over-praised unto them in England and by no knowing they shall drink water here ". The troubles of the colony were increased in 1622 when there was a massacre by the Indians, and more than a quarter of the white inhabitants were killed. Eleven were killed at Berkeley, and the plantation was more or less abandoned.

John Woodliff appears to have survived the massacre as in 1626 his name is in a list of patents sent to England, and he is said to hold 550 acres in the territory of Great Weyanoke.

A New Duke of Buckingham

The title of Duke of Buckingham had been dormant since 1521 when Edward Stafford was beheaded on Tower Hill. It was revived for George Villiers[16], favourite of James I, and friend of his son, Prince Charles. He was created Baron of Bletchley and Viscount Villiers in 1616, Earl of Buckingham in 1616, Marquess of Buckingham in 1617, his mother was made Countess of Buckingham for life in 1618, and in 1625 he became Duke of Buckingham. He was given land worth £80,000 and appointed to various offices including that of Lord High Admiral in 1619.

Handsome, witty and accomplished, the duke won the doting love of the king, the affection of the prince, and the dislike and eventual hatred of most other Englishmen. In 1623 he and Prince Charles went to Spain to try to arrange the highly unpopular marriage of Charles to the Infanta Maria. Their failure to achieve the marriage gave Villiers some temporary popularity.

When Charles I came to power he had trouble with his parliaments. In 1625 the first parliament was dissolved when it attacked the Duke of Buckingham and demanded the carrying through of laws against Roman Catholics. Buckingham town was represented by Sir Alexander Denton and Richard Oliver in this parliament, and by Sir Alexander Denton and Sir John Smith in the parliament of 1626, which impeached the Duke of Buckingham, and was dissolved by the king.

Charles protected his friend through many storms, which parliament attributed to Villiers' abuse of his excessive power; but on the morning of August 23rd, 1628 the duke was stabbed by a naval lieutenant, John Felton, who was hailed as a hero.

The second Duke of Buckingham of the Villiers line, born on 30th of January, 1628, was only a few months old when his father died, and was brought up with the princes, later Charles II and James II.

King or Parliament ?

Parliament steadily became more opposed to the king. The time was coming when people would have to stand up and be counted.

Stowe Manor had been leased by Peter Temple in 1571 and 1572. On his death in 1578 his son, John had taken over the estates, and by successful complicated business transactions, in 1589 he found an opportunity of converting the lease into full ownership. The estate was inherited by his son, Thomas, in 1603 on his father's death. The Temple family were now established as landed gentry, and Thomas Temple was one of the first baronets created on the foundation of the order by James I—he bought a title. He was also the husband of Hester Sandys, the father of six sons and nine daughters; it is said that his wife had 700 descendants before she died ! Sir Thomas impoverished himself because of the marriage portions needed for his daughters, and the expenses of his sons.

---

[16] " Encyclopaedia Britannica ", Buckingham, George Villiers.
Lipscomb II, page 551, et seq.

He was sued by his eldest son, Peter, who claimed in his marriage settlement some land that his father had sold to relieve his debts.

Sir Peter inherited the estate in 1630, when his father gave up the lands and went to live with one of his daughters. In his position as High Sheriff of Buckinghamshire, Sir Peter had the thankless task of collecting £4,500 in Ship Money from the county. His task included assessing contributions and collecting the money, much of which had to come from his friends, As, like all other sheriffs, he found it impossible to get in all the money, he was reprimanded by the Council and summoned before the King. His saddening experience as sheriff made him decide to stand with his neighbours, against the king, and he did this by entering parliament as the member for Buckingham.

In 1633 Sir Thomas Denton of Gawcott died. He had been M.P. for Buckingham in 1603, 1614 and 1620, and was succeeded by his son, Sir Alexander Denton, who partnered Sir Peter Temple in parliament in 1639 and 1640. These two men, as members of parliament, might be expected to side with parliament in any fighting.

At Lenborough Manor, Richard, the son of Richard Ingoldsby married Elizabeth Cromwell in 1613. Elizabeth was the daughter of Sir Oliver Cromwell, and cousin of the Oliver Cromwell who was later Protector of England. When the father, Richard, died in 1635, the son inherited the property and was knighted soon afterwards. The Ingoldsbys had married into the parliamentary cause, which Richard, Elizabeth and their numerous family would be expected to support.

Bourton Manor was held by Francis Poulton, who, according to Willis, " being a weak and bigotted papist, and travelling to Rome, fell into the hands of Richard Minshull, Esq., of Essex, who, advancing certain sums of money for his accommodation, acquired possession of the estate, and at a considerable expense is reported to have, circ. 1628, enclosed the Hamlet, and obtained a formal conveyance of the Lordship to himself and his heirs, subject to certain pensions ".

Richard Minshull was knighted by Charles I at Theobalds, a royal residence, on 11th December, 1626, and being honoured by the king, might be expected to support him.

Castle House was owned by the Lambert family. As we have seen, in 1607 John Lambert bought out the claim of Theophilus Adams, and when he died in 1611 was succeeded by his son William, who, with his wife Mary, did so much to improve the house. William's son, John inherited the house when his father died in 1626, and six years later John's sister, May was the owner, marrying first John Crawley of Someries, Luton, then Edward, son and heir of Sir Harvey Bagot. Castle House was part of the borough of Buckingham, a borough which had been heavily assessed for

Ship-Money. A schedule of levies for Ship-Money referred to by Roundell[17] shows Banbury, Burrow and Parish assessed at £40, Brackley £50, Buckingham £70 and Oxford £100. Buckinghamshire was a parliamentary stronghold; John Hampden had represented Wendover in the three early parliaments of Charles I and in the Short Parliament and the Long Parliament, and he had great influence in the county. Little Buckingham was surrounded by supporters of Parliament, and had been assessed heavily for ship-money. The town could reasonably be expected to follow the rest of the county and oppose the king.

[17] Roundell page 15.

CHAPTER V

THE CIVIL WAR[1]

WHEN England was dividing itself into those for the King and those for Parliament, most of Buckinghamshire sided with Parliament. Buckingham town showed its independence by being loyal to the King. The country gentlemen who lived nearby were drawn to one side or the other, by loyalties or family ties. Men who had visited each other and been good friends suddenly became enemies—to the death, and to the destruction of each other's homes.

Sir Peter Temple declared for Parliament and went to Aylesbury to serve on a committee for raising troops for the parliamentary cause. Sir Richard Ingoldsby of Lenborough went too, though possibly for different reasons from Sir Peter, as he had married into the Cromwell family. Other Parliamentary supporters were Sir Edward Tyrell of Thornton Hall, Mr. Purefoy of Shalstone, who was living at his seat at Wadley in Berkshire, and Thomas and James Chaloner of Claydon House, trustees of a young ward. They paid £200 to the parliamentary funds to obtain a release for the ward from all future parliamentary claims.

The King was not without supporters. They included Mr. Robert Busby of Addington House, who was living at Gray's Inn in London, Mr. Bate of Maids Moreton House, whose brother was Rector of Maids Moreton when Colonel Purefoy destroyed the ornaments and stained glass of the church. Other Royalists were Thomas, Lord Wenham of Twyford, Sir Alexander Denton of Hillesden (although he had been an M.P.), Sir Richard Minshull of Bourton House, who had been knighted by the King, and was personally attached to him.

Sir Edmund Verney of Claydon House became the Royal Standard Bearer, losing his life at Edgehill, his hand severed from his body, but still clutching a piece of the standard. His son, Ralph declared for Parliament, but spent much of the war in exile in France after refusing the Covenant in 1643.

In August 1642 Sir Richard Minshull equipped ten mounted troopers and set out to join the king's army in the north, leaving his wife and servants to look after Bourton House. His neighbours

---

[1] This chapter has been based on two lectures by the Rev. H. Roundell.

They are:—1. A lecture read before the Members of the Buckingham Literary and Scientific Institution under the title of: " Buckingham Town, Buckingham People, and their Neighbours during the Civil Wars ".

2. " Some Account of the Town of Buckingham ", which also was read to the Members of the Buckingham Literary and Scientific Institution.

with the parliamentary forces at Aylesbury decided to teach him a lesson. An example would be made of Sir Richard Minshull, so that all around Buckingham would see what happened to those who supported the King.

On August 18th, 1642 " Lord Brooke, with a large body of troops and artillery came to Boreton; the house was defenceless, and he gained speedy entrance ". The house, which has since disappeared, was strongly built of stone, in the shape of a letter T, three stories high and with large windows—a comfortable house to live in, but not one to be defended, especially by a woman and house-servants.

Lady Minshull surrendered, the soldiers entered and broke up the furniture, drank the wine, and even dug up the wine cellar to look for treasure. They ripped the lead from the roofs, used books to heat the ovens to cook their food, broke doors, windows, glass, killed the pigeons in the pigeon-house, tried to burn the house, then sold or killed the sheep and lambs. Lady Minshull was guarded, her servants threatened till some fled; the neighbours were so threatened " to extort confessions from them where Sir Richard Minshull was, or where any of his goods were conveyed that some fainted for fear, some fell mad, and others dyed ".

On October 23rd there was the indecisive battle of Edge Hill; support for the King strengthened in the West Country and in Wales, while parliamentary support grew in London and the surrounding counties. In March 1643 peace proposals were made —armies would occupy their present positions, the king's quarters would be at Brill, and his troops were not to advance into Buckinghamshire beyond Brill. The parliamentary forces were not to move beyond their garrison at Aylesbury. However, the negotiations failed, and Prince Rupert made a dashing though unsuccessful attack on Aylesbury. Some of the king's generals with 400 men marched on Winslow, captured 40 horses, marched on to Swanbourne where they captured 40 ' Musqueteers ', and demonstrated that Buckinghamshire was not entirely in parliamentary hands.

A letter from John Wittewrong and Thomas Tyrrill (Tyrell) to Colonel Hampden and Colonel Goodwyn was read in both Houses of Parliament on 18th May, 1643. It told of the lack of parliamentary forces in Buckinghamshire, the outrages that the royalists were committing, including the burning of Swanbourne, and as the final indignity, said, " For they now are so strong that they quarter at Buckingham and where they please, in those parts without resistance ".

Buckingham was not a garrison town during the Civil War, but was occupied by the sides alternately, the poor townspeople producing food and money for whichever troops demanded it.

The royalist success at Winslow and Swanbourne was an encouragement to them to advance to other parts of the county. In June 1643 Prince Rupert marched to Buckingham as is told in

" Mercurius Aulicus," the Royalist newspaper, under the heading " Buckingham, June 30th Friday,—Prince Rupert with a considerable strength of horse and Dragoons came this day to Buckingham and found such entertainment in that part of the Country, that the people came in freely to him and confessed how much they had been formerly seduced by the powerful sorceries of Hampden, Goodwin and the rest of that combination, desired to be restored to His Majesty's favour, and to be reckoned in the list of his dutifull and obedient subjects, professing (as a testimonie of their future loyaltie) their readinesse to submit to such contributions as His Highnesse should thinke fit to impose upon them ".

Rupert arrived in Buckingham on the Friday, and by Saturday night a parliamentary cavalry force left Aylesbury under Colonel Middleton and Sir Philip Stapleton intending to surprise Rupert and his troops. Rupert was surprised—he was on his way to church when he heard the news that the enemy was at Padbury. Possibly Rupert continued calmly to church, but he arranged that Sir Charles Lucas should ride out to Padbury with some troopers. Sir Charles conccaled his men behind hedges near Bint Hill (Bent Hill ?), and surprised Stapleton's force by a front and flank attack. The Parliamentary troops panicked and fled, pursued by the Royalists to Westhill Brook near Padbury, where there were more Parliamentary forces to support them.

The Royalists won that little skirmish, but when the Earl of Essex marched towards Buckingham with an army of Parliamentary troops to do battle with Rupert, the prince retired to Banbury, leaving the townsfolk to wonder how they would fare when the next force occupied the town. Essex sent Colonel Middleton to clear the town of Royalists troops, then the Parliamentary army marched to Great Brickhill, then to Stony Stratford where they joined " Lord Grey, Colonel Cromwell and others ".

Hillesden House

Towcester was fortified by Prince Rupert, Newport Pagnell was captured by Parliament, and an expedition was sent from Newport Pagnell under Captain Abercromby to cut off royalist stragglers around Winslow and Buckingham, which was the only place in the county supporting the King. A few Royalist soldiers were at Buckingham and others at Hillesden House, home of Sir Alexander Denton, at this time. These troops were under Colonel Smith, who was trying to collect supplies there—some supplies probably coming from Buckingham.

Abercromby, who was at Addington, wrote to the Earl of Essex on January 15th, 1644, telling of how he went to Winslow then, " I whild about and tuke bukingham in my way brought five of the townsmen with me whereof on was the balli of the town and on other was the father to on of the runaway captaines on Lambert and the other three keept them presoners until they payd some arrears due to the steat ". He also said that he wished to occupy Hillesden House, which he later did, and stayed there about a month. While there he sent out warrants to provide himself and his troops with money. One warrant went to the Constables and Inhabitants of Brackley, who ignored it, as they were between the king's garrison at Banbury, Colonel Smith at Westbury and Abercromby at Hillesden. Abercromby decided to collect the money in person, but when returning to Hillesden he encountered a Royalist party at Westbury. Abercromby was pursued by Captain Dayrell, captured with fourteen of his troopers and taken to Westbury, apparently leaving Hillesden House vacant.

About the middle of February, Sir Alexander Denton decided to fortify his house. He, Colonel Smith and a large number of troops arrived there and started work. They planned an earthwork and ditch around the house and church, and a high mound with artillery on its sides, commanding the approaches on all sides. This would have been a well-fortified house, as strong as any in the county, but as there were Parliamentary spies all around, progress of the work was reported to the Governor of Newport Pagnell, who wrote it in his private despatch book and sent word to London.

Work progressed with the help of the 1,000 men employed. Things were going well until Colonel Smith led a party of dragoons and horses to Aylesbury, and brought back 100 cattle, 30 or 40 horses and as many pigs. This precipitated trouble, as most of the cattle were stolen from a Mr. Burton, a tenant on Hampden's estate, and he complained and demanded compensation from Parliament. The committee at Aylesbury thought it time to deal with Hillesden House, as a strong Royalist force there could interfere with their communications with Newport Pagnell. Three hundred men set out for Hillesden House, arriving there at 7.0 a.m. on the 28th February, but the defenders were alert, so the Parliamentarians attacked a cottage and a barn and returned to Aylesbury.

Sir Samuel Luke, Governor of Newport Pagnell organised the next attempt, helped by his spies' information. He took 2000 men from Newport Pagnell, marched them to Claydon and rested them there on the night of the 3rd of March. The next morning he surrounded Hillesden House, called on the defenders to surrender, and when his terms were refused, he attacked. There were only 263 defenders, against an attacking force of 2,000, and the attackers soon over-ran the earthworks. The defenders retreated to the church and house, but on a second assault, Colonel Smith realised that resistance was useless, so he surrendered himself and his men " on promise of quarter ".

A large number of prisoners were taken, many were killed after the surrender, as was stated even in the " Parliamentary Scout ", an anti-Royalist paper. Those killed were buried in one big grave in Hillesden church-yard.

The surviving prisoners, including Sir Alexander and Colonel Smith, were taken to Padbury, where Sir Alexander was kept all day, to watch his house being burnt. His sister, who was his housekeeper since his wife's death, was left with no home, and with eight or nine children to look after. Her request to be left at least a few cows to give milk for the children was refused, and we are not told what happened to her.

We do know what happened to some of the prisoners. The common soldiers were exchanged at Newport, where all were taken, but the more important men were sent to London. Sir Alexander and Colonel Smith had both been Members of Parliament, and had been expelled from the House for helping the king. Ten days after their surrender they were summoned to the Bar of the Commons, and after defending themselves, Colonel Smith was committed a prisoner in the Poltrey Compter, and Sir Alexander was sent to the Tower. Neither were to be exchanged without the permission of the Commons.

Sir Alexander Denton had a particularly hard time during the war, as his house was burnt, his estates taken from him, his brother-in-law, Sir Edmund Verney was killed at Edge Hill, and he himself was in the Tower. While there, he heard that his son had been killed in battle. This news, and the confinement in the Tower caused his health to deteriorate, and he asked Parliament if he could be allowed to leave the Tower. He was allowed to go to Lord Petre's house, still guarded, and he died in London and was buried at Hillesden on the 5th of January, 1645.

Cromwell's Visit to Buckingham

Three days after the defeat of the Royalists at Hillesden, Cromwell marched to Buckingham, intending to assemble a large force there and attack Banbury or Oxford. We do not know where he stayed in Buckingham, but his troops would be billeted in houses around the town. Cromwell did not go to Oxford, but instead joined the Earl of Essex and his army at Thame, so that all the parliamentary forces had left Buckingham by the end of March.

Captain Dayrell, a Royalist, then occupied the town and extracted money from the weary inhabitants to help the king's cause. He withdrew soon so that there were no Royalist forces nearer than Oxford and Banbury.

King Charles I Visits Buckingham

For a fortnight there was quiet in the town. No doubt people were busy trying to get the place cleared up once again. Early in the morning of the 22nd of June, 1644 the King and his army arrived in Buckingham by the Tingewick Road, and with him came 4,000 foot soldiers, 4,000 horse and ten pieces of artillery. Yet again troops were quartered in the houses and inns, yet again food was commandeered, but this time the King had come, and as the town was an island of Royalists in a sea of Buckinghamshire Parliamentarians, the town would celebrate. Some of the leaders in the celebrations would be Thomas Napton, the bailiff, Mr. Whitby, the Vicar, and Mr. Yeomans, master of the Royal Latin School.

Spies were there too, and Leonard Sharpe sent to the enemy on the same day, details of the units in the Royalist army as they entered the town. " The troopers have all of them swords, and every other man a pistol ".

The crowd at the Horse Fair would push and jostle as they waited for the King to enter Castle House, walking up to the door in his gleaming armour. Buckingham was honoured. Some would stay in the streets, but many would go home to protect the remains of their belongings from the army which always took what it wanted.

That night there was a Council of War in Castle House, where two plans were discussed. Some members of the Council proposed a march on the Associated Counties of Northampton, Bedford and Cambridge, from which Parliament largely obtained supplies of men and provisions. Another plan was to march northwards to join Prince Rupert, then with the united Royalist armies to completely crush Sir William Waller in Worcestershire, and Lord Essex in Dorset. A third proposal was to march to London, which was almost undefended, and attack Parliament in its own House. As usual, the King was undecided and stayed for three precious days in Buckingham.

While here he was joined by Prince Charles, and he received news of the birth of his daughter, the Princess Henrietta, at Exeter.

After his three days of hesitation, the King and his army set off for Bletchingdon, near Oxford, but the King changed his mind and quartered his troops at Brackley. Three days later he fought the indecisive battle of Cropredy Bridge.

After Cropredy Bridge, Sir William Fairfax and his army came to Buckingham, and he came again in May 1645.

During the Civil War the town was not besieged or heavily damaged, but the people suffered the uncertainty of what tomorrow would bring, and too often, it brought more soldiers.

CHAPTER VI

A SECOND CHARTER

The Commonwealth 1649-1660

THE war was over and the King defeated. During the Commonwealth Buckingham would not be the gay place of earlier days. The bulls would not be baited in the Bull Ring, and any fairs would be for business and not for fun. Buckingham had supported the losing side, and those concerned would probably want to lie low.

Thomas Napton[1] had been bailiff in 1644 when the king visited the town, and was elected again in 1646, but not during the Commonwealth. There may be no significance in this, as some other men were bailiffs during both the war and the Commonwealth. Will. Atton was bailiff in 1642, 1649 and 1657, Ben Yeomans in 1645 and 1655, Will. Stevens in 1647 and 1656 and Will. Reeve in 1651 and 1661. The last three burgesses had a gap of nine or ten years between their turns as bailiff, an unexplained feature that is repeated in other men who were bailiffs. Will. Stevens or someone of the same name was bailiff again in 1672, 25 years after his first term, meaning that he must have been a relatively young man when elected a burgess, as one would suppose that the bailiff was elected from experienced burgesses. George Dancer also, was elected a burgess while quite young, as he was bailiff in 1669, 1679, 1687 and 1693.

Thomas Whitby, who had been Vicar of Buckingham before the war, had died in 1646 and been succeeded by William Stilton. There is no mention of his being replaced by a Puritan minister during the Commonwealth, as happened in other places, and, unlike 2,000 Puritan clergy, he was not replaced by an Anglican clergyman at the Restoration, so he must have swayed with the wind. He did not obtain a legal title to his position of vicar until 31st July, 1662, after the Restoration, when he was presented by Dr. William Denton, Edward Fust, Alexander Denton and George Woodward[2].

Some Royalists suffered for their loyalty. Sir Richard Minshull[3] of Bourton was one of these unfortunate people. His house had been ransacked during the war, and his estates had been taken from him by Parliament. He negotiated an agreement with Parliament, paying £1,378 for the return of his estates, but Lipscomb quotes an opinion that his " loss was not less than £2,000 ".

The Dentons of Hillesden also suffered for their Royalist loyalty[4].

[1] Lipscomb II, page 567.
[2] Lipscomb II, page 574.
[3] Lipscomb II, page 590.   Sheahan page 249.
[4] Roundell—" Buckingham during the Civil War ", page 25.

The ones who supported Parliament fared rather differently. As was mentioned earlier, the Ingoldsbys of Lenborough had married into the Protector's family. The second Sir Richard Ingoldsby married Elizabeth Cromwell, daughter of Sir Oliver Cromwell of Hitchinbrook, Huntingdonshire, who was an uncle of Oliver Cromwell, the Protector. This meant that Elizabeth was a cousin of the Protector. Francis, the first son of Sir Richard and Elizabeth was M.P. for Buckingham in the Commonwealth Parliaments of 1653, 1656 and 1659[5].

The second son was Richard[6], who was educated at Thame Grammar School, and at the beginning of the Civil War was a captain in Hampden's regiment. By 1645 he was a colonel of a regiment of foot soldiers in the ' New Model ' regiment which sided with the army in the quarrel between the army and Parliament, and one of the first regiments to demand the punishment of the king. Richard Ingoldsby was appointed one of the judges at the trial of the king, does not seem to have attended the trial, but signed the death warrant. He committed himself very firmly against the Royalists.

He had been an M.P. before this time, representing Wendover in 1647, and according to the National Dictionary of Biography, but not Lipscomb, representing Buckingham in 1654 and 1656. In November 1652 he was chosen as a member of the Council of State, and in 1657 he was summoned to Cromwell's House of Lords. When Richard Cromwell succeeded his father, Oliver, as Protector of England, he was soon in trouble with the army officers, who wanted to overthrow him and control Parliament themselves. Richard Ingoldsby vigorously supported Richard Cromwell, who was his kinsman, and suffered for it by losing his command when Richard Cromwell was dismissed from being Protector. When Richard Ingoldsby saw that the Restoration was imminent, he got in touch with the king's agents, to try to better his own position as a regicide, one who had signed the death warrant of Charles II's father.

Another son of Richard and Elizabeth Ingoldsby, Sir Henry Ingoldsby[7], commanded a regiment in Ireland, under Oliver Cromwell, and represented the counties of Limerick, Kerry and Clare in the Parliaments of 1654, 1656 and 1659. When in 1659 there was trouble between the army and parliament, he seized Windsor Castle for Parliament, who thanked him for his loyalty. He had the double honour of being created a baronet by the Protector and by Charles II.

Sir Peter Temple of Stowe had been M.P. for Buckingham in the last two Parliaments of Charles I and on the Parliamentary side in the war. In 1649 Peter Temple was named as one of the judges for the king's trial. but he refused to serve—unlike two of his

---

[5] Lipscomb II, page 560. Sheahan page 251.
[6] [7] National Dictionary of Biography.

relations who signed the death warrant, and as regicides died in prison after the Restoration.

Stowe estate would be easily raided and pillaged during the war, especially by troops staying in Buckingham. Even in 1662 the vicarage was still fallen down, and only one person, Mr. Miller was living in Boycott village. In 1649 Sir Peter enclosed 200 acres of land, possibly without any local opposition, as the people of Stowe and Boycott villages may already have moved to Lamport and Dadford. His troubles were not yet over, as he became deep in debt—about £24,000 (nearly half a million by today's values), and a harsh settlement was worked out but not legalised, when he died.

George Villiers, 2nd Duke of Buckingham of the Villiers line[8], had been brought up with the princes who were later to be Charles II and James II. He and his brother fought on the Royalist side in the Civil War, his brother being killed. He joined Charles in exile in Holland, and according to Bishop Gilbert Burnet, proceeded to initiate Charles into the vices that he had himself acquired. His influence over Charles waned after the defeat at Worcester in 1651 of Charles' army, on his attempted return to England—a return that Villiers had encouraged, and the Scottish Presbyterians had aided.

He must have decided that Charles stood little chance of regaining the throne, as he now wondered how he could regain his estates that had been taken from him by Parliament. He returned to England—Commonwealth England—in the summer of 1657, and by September he married Mary Fairfax, the daughter of the Parliamentary general, Lord Fairfax, who had been granted a large part of the Villiers estates for his services to Parliament. This bare-faced change of sides and equally bare-faced marrying to regain his land, did not achieve the results he wished. Oliver Cromwell saw this manoeuvre as a Royalist-Presbyterian plot against the government, and Villiers was thrown into the Tower. The influence of his father-in-law and the timely death of the Protector saved him from probable execution. He was released on February 23rd, 1659 and stayed at his father-in-law's house.

Restoration and a New Charter

When Charles II was asked to return to England as king, there would be rejoicings in Buckingham town. Those royalists who had lost land during the Commonwealth would hope for its return, and those who had received the land would wait fearfully, hoping that they might be overlooked.

By the Act of Indemnity and Oblivion, Charles and his country attempted to settle the troubles caused by the Civil War and the Commonwealth. Lands confiscated during and after the war were

[8] " Encyclopaedia Britannica "—Buckingham, Duke of.

restored to their former owners, but lands sold by Royalists to cover the fines imposed by Parliament, stayed with their new owners.

George Villiers changed sides once again and greeted his king as he landed at Dover. His reception was understandably cool, the amazing thing being that after a few months of gay life in Restoration England, he was once again in Royal favour. His charm must have been much greater than his loyalty.

The Act of Indemnity and Oblivion pardoned all who had fought against the king—all except the regicides. Those who had signed the death warrant of Charles I would wait in dread of the consequences. Sir Richard Ingoldsby[9] was one of these; when questioned on his part in the death of the king, he said that his signature was extorted by force, " Cromwell taking his hand in his, and putting the pen between his fingers, with his own hand, writ Richard Ingoldsby, he making all the resistance he could ". But the name is said to be very clearly written, showing no sign of constraint and is accompanied by the Ingoldsby's family seal.

The king did not pardon him or promise that Ingoldsby would not suffer in some way for signing the death warrant. But Ingoldsby was not sent to the Tower, the fate of some of the regicides. Instead, he was allowed to earn his pardon by services to the king. These included putting down the intended rising of John Lambert, former Parliamentary general, who opposed the king's return. Ingoldsby captured and brought him triumphantly to London, was thanked by the Commons on 22nd April, 1660 and was spared the Tower. He played his hand so well that at Charles' coronation on 20th April, 1661 he was made a Knight of the Bath, and later became M.P. for Aylesbury in four Parliaments of this king.

As already mentioned, Sir Henry Ingoldsby helped in smoothing the way for the Restoration and in 1661 was created a baronet. The eldest brother, Sir Francis Ingoldsby had inherited the Lenborough estate in 1656. Browne Willis gives his history most concisely, " As to Francis Ingoldsby, the eldest son of Sir Richard, who succeeded him in his Estate; he was returned Member of Parliament for Buckingham in the Years 1654, 1656, and 1658-9, in the Rump Parliaments; and living at Lenborough in too profuse a Manner, his Wife also, as it was reported, being extravagant and vain, they run out the Estate, and disparked the Park made by his Grandfather; and having deeply mortgaged it, they retired to London, about 1673, where he deceased October 1st, 1681, being then a pensioner in the Charter-House; to which he was admitted 1679: and his children, whose names were Francis, Richard, Elizabeth, Anne, Lucy, and Lettice, were reduced to Poverty ".

Before Sir Francis' death the mortgaged estate at Lenborough was made over to his steward, William Robinson, who lived there, dying in 1696, and leaving the estate to his relation William Robin-

---

[9] National Dictionary of Biography—Ingoldsby.

son. He also left " an Annual Benefaction to Cloathe two poor Men with Blue Coats ".

Sir Richard Temple (1634-1697) inherited Stowe estate and his father's massive debts which he had paid off by 1656, mortgages being taken out on half a dozen properties. After the Restoration he was M.P. for Buckingham and retained his seat for the rest of his life, except for 1678-9, when he was defeated through the influence of the Duke of Buckingham, George Villiers. By persistently attacking the king's chief minister, Clarendon, he was given the post of First Commissioner for Customs. The appointment was a bribe to make him cease his attacks. The salary of £2,000, promptly paid, enabled him to clear the mortgages, and along with a wealthy marriage, to rebuild and furnish Stowe House, and rent a town house in London.

The restoration of Charles II to the throne brought changes to many people. Many Puritan clergy were removed and replaced by Anglicans. Our Vicar, William Stilton did not suffer in this way, but benefited in 1660 when a new vicarage was built on the Field of Walnuts, some land that had been given to the church in 1445. This is the present vicarage, in Church Street, conveniently near the site of the old church. The original E-shaped building has been altered in 1812 and added to in 1854. The present dining-room, facing the river, is a later addition, being built over what was originally a garden. Two fireplaces are made of local marble, which was quarried in the 19th century.

This vicarage and some other livings were endowed with an estate in Essex by Dr. William Clark, Dean of Winchester, who died in 1679. This gave about £15 per year to each of the incumbents.

Buckingham Tokens[10]

Between 1649 and 1672 there was a shortage of small coins for change, and tradesmen and innkeepers throughout England issued their own coins. These were used only locally and often had the name of the tradesman stamped on one side. Browne Willis was one of the first collectors of trade tokens and his collection of 1,100 tokens is now in the Ashmolean Museum at Oxford, and others of his coins are in the Bodleian. He describes the issue of the tokens, " Anno 1649, or somewhat earlier, in the times of anarchy and confusion, private persons took upon them to coin their own farthings or halfpence, and so did till 1672 when by proclamation this kind of money was descried and the king's copper farthings and halfpence took place. This practice first began in London where farthings only were struck till after 1660 . . . . and from hence they advanced to halfpennies and pennies. And, as these had been universally stamped by shop-keepers and traders of the greatest note in almost all the market towns and in several

[10] Harrison page 82. Dragon of Whaddon by J. G. Jenkins, page 134 et seq.

Market Hill and the Old Gaol, Buckingham over 50 years ago.

(R. & H. Chapman)

Buckingham Old Town Hall

villages with the impress of the persons' names, signs, or coats of arms of their companies, and some few with their family arms, so cities, towns, parish officers, companies, and collieries minted theirs likewise and gave sanction to their currency ".

Tokens of this type were issued at Buckingham, and Harrison says that Mr. Ratcliff of Olney had a collection of them. The tokens known to have been issued include these:

Wm. Atton, Draper in Buckingham   ...   1663
     (He, or someone of the same name was bailiff in 1630, 1642, 1649 and 1657).

John Kew, his halfpenny, Buckingham ...		1668
John Hartlee	,, ...	1650
John Rennals	,, ...	1668
John Hartley, Jr.	,, ...	1665
George Robins, Mercer	,, ...	no date
Peter Reynolds	,, ...	no date
Elizabeth Crawley	,, ...	1668

The token issued by John Hartlee has his name and the year, 1650, in a circle on one side, with a picture of a heart in the centre. On the other side is J.H. in the centre, with IN BUCKINGHAM round the edge. That of George Robins has a sheep in the centre of one side with GEORGE ROBINS * In * round the edge; on the other side is G.R. in the centre and BUCKINGHAM * MERCER round the edge. John Rennals' token has HIS HALFE PENNY in the centre of one side, with OF BUCKINGHAM round the edge.

Cheerful Buckingham[11]

After the Restoration George Villiers and the other local gentry used to meet at Buckingham when they were staying at their country houses. Villiers had a seat at Whaddon and would come to Buckingham for a game of bowls. A new bowling-green had been laid out on Castle Hill, covering some of the ruins of the castle. There would be a wonderful view of the surrounding country from the green for the gentlemen to admire between games. The bowling in the open-air with a hill-top breeze would give them a good appetite and an even better thirst, which would be quenched at the Trolley Hall in Castle Street. This is described by Browne Willis as " A large Room for the Entertainment of the Gentlemen of the County ". Trolley Hall and the bowling-green were two of Mr. Henry Robinson's enterprises. He was a lace-buyer, and he also set up a stage-coach to go from Buckingham to London and back, the whole journey in 4 days. Roundell says " an undertaking, which when all the opposition made to the introduction of coaches as a means of travelling is taken into account, proves him to have been a man of both courage and energy. Robinson's day and night

[11] V.C.H. Bucks III, page 472. Roundell page 25. Harrison page 41.

coach to London, was one of the earliest of such conveyances, .for, in 1672, only six stage coaches were constantly running out of London ".

The tradesmen of Buckingham would be rubbing their hands and counting their trade tokens as the borough enjoyed its position as County Town. The summer assizes seem to have been held at Buckingham once again later in the century, the judges sitting very uncomfortably in sheds erected against the ruined castle walls. Browne Willis says that the poll for the Knights of the Shire was taken on Castle Hill in 1679 when the election was adjourned to Aylesbury.

A New Town Hall

Buckingham was the scene of bribery and corruption when parliamentary elections were approaching. The bailiff and burgesses were the entire electorate, holding the fates of the candidates in their power. In the first Restoration election Francis Ingoldsby was defeated and objected to the results of the election on the grounds that the freemen of the town and not just the bailiff and burgesses, had the right of election. The decision from the Committee of Privileges, who considered the question, was that by Queen Mary's charter, the right of election was with the bailiff and burgesses only.

The Victoria History, page 478, says that this limitation of the electorate gave rise " to Buckingham occupying a unique position as a rotten borough under the influence of the Dukes of Buckingham ". George Villiers, then Duke of Buckingham, used his influence in 1678-9, when he " went himself to the town and made it his business to persuade the people not to choose Lord Latimer or Sir Richard Temple ". The persuasion may have been beer, wines, dinners or money, but whatever form it took, it was unsuccessful. The Duke's candidate, Sir Philip Tyrrel was defeated, and once again a petition was laid, this time against Sir Richard Temple's election, on the grounds that undue returns had been made by the bailiff. Lipscomb shows a double return for this election:

1678 Edw. Visc. Latimer; Rich. Temple, Bart.
Edw. Visc. Latimer; Peter Terrill, Bart.

In 1679 the sheriff suddenly changed the meeting place for county elections from Aylesbury to Buckingham, and in 1685 it was changed to Newport Pagnell, the latter change being at the suggestion of Judge Jefferies, infamous for his Bloody Assizes.

Roundell has an improbable story of heavy bribery in the elections of 1680, which seems to be a shortened version of one given by Silvester. At this election Sir Richard Temple and Sir William Smith were standing together and by fair means or foul had persuaded the bailiff and burgesses to promise them their votes. George Villiers once again interfered, asking Sir Richard Temple to use his influence with the voters to substitute Mr. Clifford, a friend of Villiers, for Sir Richard's running mate, Sir William Smith. When the word of this reached Sir William Smith he was understandably furious, and asked Mr. John Dormer, who had been M.P. in 1660 to stand with him against Sir Richard Temple and Mr. Clifford.

Sir Richard Temple, Mr. Clifford and George Villiers must have had a firm grip on the voters, as the opposing candidates found that they had to resort to really heavy bribery. They suggested to the corporation that the Town Hall was not a grand enough building for such an important town, and that they would provide a better one if elected to parliament. Silvester says that they offered £300 towards the building. At any rate, the corporation were impressed and agreed that the Town Hall was not suitable. Silvester says that by this time, six votes were promised to Sir Richard Temple and five to Mr. Dormer, so that the other two votes were vital. The bailiff and burgesses may or may not have asked Sir Richard what he was prepared to do about the Town Hall, but the story goes that Sir Richard's friends decided that action was better than words, and had £40 worth of stone and timber dumped in the market place, and promised that Sir Richard would pay half the cost of the building if he was elected. The M.P.'s for 1679 (Lipscomb) were Edw. Viscount Latimer and Richard Temple, Bart., K.B.

It may be that Silvester confused the date 1680 with 1685, as the memoirs of the Verney Family 1660 to 1694, Vol. IV, edited by Margaret Verney, 1899, give a similar story about the 1685 election.

In 1685 Sir Ralph Verney was 72 years old, but still interested in politics. He may have hesitated whether to stand again, but there was a rumour that young Alexander Denton of Hillesden would like to stand, if Sir Ralph was too infirm, and that implication was enough to decide things. Sir Ralph would stand with his cousin, Sir Richard Temple of Stowe, a combination that had won two seats for Buckingham for the Whigs in 1681. Sir Richard was unpopular with the Verneys of Claydon and the Dentons of Hillesden, as he was a scheming man, secretive in some things and too verbose in others. Two years before this, he and Edmund Verney had prepared the way for another election, by going to Buckingham and ensuring that a bailiff was chosen who was friendly to Sir Richard. Edmund Verney then said that if he had not been there with Sir Richard, " I may asseure you without Vanity That Sr Richard's greatest Ennemy Robinson Hadd Been Bayly: Whereof now Mr. Hillesdon Sr Richard's ffreind is Bayly ". This enemy was Henry Robinson, the enterprising builder of Trolley Hall and the owner of the stage coach. Edmund Verney was disgusted that Sir Richard once travelled in Robinson's coach, to " sweeten the Bitternesse of his Enemy " especially as Robinson, while in Bristol, had called Sir Richard " a Rogue & Rascall and Knave etc."

For the 1685 election, the electorate had to be sweetened. Sir Ralph Verney agreed to go along with Sir Richard Temple in spending £10 or £20 each on gifts to the poor, expenses on election day, and a dinner for the Mayor and Aldermen (the new titles) in thanks for their " love and kindness ". There were some things that he would not do, such as:—" treat the Mobile at all the Ale-houses in the Parish & to make them Drunke, perhapps a Month beforehand, as is usual in too many places uppon such occasions, I shall not Joyne in that Expence, I had rather sit still, than gaine a place in Parliament by so much debauchery ".

The Tory candidates who opposed Sir Ralph and Sir Richard, were Lord Latimer and Sir John Busby of Addington, and Bucking-ham saw a lot of all the candidates in the weeks before the election. Sir Ralph preferred to stay at home keeping warm, as it was March and there were cold winds. His sons did much of the electioneering for him, but even so he had to be in Buckingham for market days, and to visit Mr. Hugh Ethersey, the mayor, who had complained that Sir Ralph had not called on him lately, and that Sir Ralph never spent 20 shillings in Buckingham in 20 years, meaning money spent on ale.

Seven votes were needed to be sure of the election, and as there were three, including the mayor, solidly against Sir Ralph, the other ten voters were courted and bribed. One voter was arrested for debt, and as he was the Verneys' barber, they thought he would vote for them. Money was found to pay his debts, and he was released from prison and brought to Buckingham in a coach, but was cool and distant with the Verneys as he knew the value of his vote.

A report then began to go around the town that Lord Latimer had offered to lay down £300 for building a Town Hall and this offer was repeated. Lord Latimer was trying hard for votes, but so were Sir Ralph's friends and even his staff. His cook, Nicholas did some canvassing and also cooked a meal for the mayor and aldermen and their families, though he felt that his " artistic cold collations were thrown away upon thirsty Aldermen ". Sir Ralph kept himself going with coffee, and was prepared for a long fight, as the borough elections would be after those for the Knights of the Shire.

In the county elections, Lord Chief Justice Jeffreys was taking a hand. He supported the Tory candidate, Mr. Hackett, who was from near Newport Pagnell. Judge Jeffreys persuaded the sheriff to adjourn the poll from Aylesbury to Newport Pagnell, where many would vote for Mr. Hackett, and other candidates would lose votes, as many people could not travel so far to vote. Despite the move of the poll to the extreme northern end of the county, Mr. Hackett was defeated, possibly because one of the other can-didates was ready to spend £1,500 a day on the election. Sir Ralph was delighted with the result, but still worried about the borough elections, as the mayor was threatening to report one of the Whig aldermen, Dancer, a tanner, to the king for words against the Government; he and another alderman were to be turned out of the Commission of the Peace. If Dancer could be summoned to London on however trumpery a charge, the election could be held in his absence and Sir Ralph would lose his seat. Sir Ralph and his friends went to great lengths to try to prevent this, but their trouble was unnecessary, as the Corporation of Buckingham refused to join " in soe foule a practice against 2 of their brethren ".

The opposition to Sir Ralph collapsed, Sir John Busby was thrown over by his own party, Lord Latimer did not turn up on election day, Sir Ralph won 7 votes and Sir Richard Temple 12 " after which the Mayor sent for us upp into the Towne Hall, and declared the Election and sealed the Indenture or Returne with the Towne Seale and then all 12 Electors put their hands to it, and delivered it to one to carry to the Sheriffs tomorrow morning ".

The rest of the townsfolk had wanted a vote too, and " the Populace went to the Towne Hall and civilly demanded the Pole for my Ld Latimer and my Cozen Greenfield of Foscut, but the Mayor told them hee could not grant it, soe they went away and poled a little & then separated without noyse or tumult ".

One can see where the story of the building of the town hall came from, and although Buckingham at this time had a town hall of sorts, it cannot have been a very grand building, as Thomas Baskerville about this time had reported that there was no town hall here. The truth may be that Sir Ralph Verney paid for a building, as in " The Verneys of Claydon " it says of him, " He had the satisfaction of feeling that he had left Buckingham the better for his long political connection with it. He had, as Mr. Butterfield writes, ' erected a lasting monument of his munificence ' in the town hall, often promised by rival candidates, and forgotten when the elections were over, built about 1685 at the expense of Sir Ralph Verney ".

The story is not however, reported by Browne Willis, who wrote his book in 1755, and it is probable that he would have revelled in the tale if he had heard it.

According to the honorary borough archivist, the town hall which was built, possibly as a result of a parliamentary election was the building described by Silvester, as erected on pillars, the lower part open and used as a market house, the upper part a large room called the Town Hall. This building is also described from memory by James Bennett[12], a veterinary surgeon of Stowe, who was probably the James Bennett who was born at Stowe in 1734 and died in 1816. He remembered that the assizes were held in the upper part. This building was between the White Hart and the present Lloyds Bank, as shown in Jeffrey's map.

[12] Harrison's papers.

At the back of Harrison's book there is a note that in 1783 " The Corporation met at the ' Cobham Arms Inn ', as the old Sessions House was pulled down and the new Town Hall not finished ". The " old Sessions House " was the one built in 1680 or 1685, and the " new Town Hall " is the one now standing, which was built in 1783. Sir Nikolaus Pevsner in his " Buildings of England ", dates the red brick facade as of the 1780's.

The upper part of the new Town Hall has been used for elections, public meetings, dances and as a Court Room; the summer assizes for the county were held there or in the old Sessions House from 1748 to July 1848[13]. The ground floor has been used as offices for the borough and county magistrates, a council chamber and billiard room.

A New Charter

For some years King Charles II had been having trouble with his parliaments. Lord Shaftesbury and his supporters wished to exclude Charles' Catholic brother James from succession to the throne. This group, the Whigs, wanted to exclude even James' Protestant children, Mary and Anne, and Mary's Protestant husband, William of Orange, from the throne. They claimed succession for the Duke of Monmouth, illegitimate son of Charles, and likely to be easily influenced by Shaftesbury.

Charles dissolved parliament and summoned another one to Oxford in March 1681, away from the London mob. This parliament was dissolved within eight days, and for the next four years Charles ruled without a parliament, having obtained a promise of £400,000 from Louis XIV of France.

While he had no parliament, the king dealt with the main support of the Whigs, which lay in the municipal corporations. Charles deprived London and over 60 other cities and boroughs of their charters, using various pretexts. The new charters that were given allowed the crown more control over the corporation and the election of M.P.'s, the object being to reduce the number of Whigs in parliament and allow James to follow Charles on the throne. " Buckingham had received such a charter in the previous July; the two borough members were elected by the Mayor and twelve Aldermen," Lady Verney wrote in her Memoirs of the Verney Family, speaking of 1685.

The arrival in Buckingham of the new Charter was reported in the " London Gazette " of August 28th to September 1st, 1684, as a joyful event[14], with " Bells ringing, Waits and other Musick playing and the Streets being crowded with People who expressed great satisfaction . . . . And then Sir Richard Temple declared to them the great Honor and Advantages they received by their New Charter, the King having been pleased to incorporate them by the

[13] Sheahan page 242.
[14] Harrison's papers.

name of the Mayor and Aldermen of the Loyal Borough and Parish of Buckingham, and to grant them two new Fairs . . . . and every Saturday a Market for live Cattle, with many additions to their former Privileges ".

This Charter was written in Latin, and as far as can be ascertained there is no English translation. With the help of the Rev. C. M. Devine of the Franciscan College, the Charles Charter was studied and compared with the Mary Charter. The two were found to be similar in many respects, both in the arrangement of the subjects and in the privileges granted. Towards the end of the Charles Charter it is stated that any privileges which were in the Mary Charter and were omitted from the Charles Charter (but not abrogated in the Charles Charter), might be applied for and would be granted. The " Prison or Gaol " was omitted, and there is no mention of the Leet Court or Frankpledge.

In the Charles Charter the Mayor was elected in the same way as the Bailiff had been elected, but was to take office on " the day of the moon next following the Feast of St. Michael the Archangel and from that day for a year ". He was to be a Justice of the Peace, as the Bailiff had been.

The Aldermen were elected for life as the Burgesses had been. The two M.P.s were elected in the same way . . . . " The Mayor and Aldermen to elect, choose and nominate two discreet and honest men . . . . "

The corporation could make its own bye-laws, and there was a market and cattle-market. Two fairs were granted, but on different days from the Mary Charter.

A three-weekly court could be held, to hear and terminate cases of debts etc. not exceeding £40 in value. The limit in the Mary Charter had been £5. The borough appears to have been given more responsibility in this respect.

A new part was included granting the borough the " special permission of the lawful power and authority of having and receiving in perpetuity, manors, messuages, lands, tenements, meadows, fields, grazing grounds, tithes and returns not exceeding the clear annual value of £100 ". This seems to be a new privilege.

There appears to be only one restriction which is greater in the Charles Charter than in the Mary Charter. This was that any Alderman was to have lands to the clear annual value of £5 and had to be a householder, (the value was 13s. 4d. in the Mary Charter, and no mention of the householder) or was to have goods and chattels to the value of £100, and was to pay " scot and lot ". (This was £20 in the Mary Charter, and no mention of " scot and lot ".)

This means that the Mayor and Aldermen would, in general, be wealthier people than the bailiff and burgesses had been. They might be expected to elect fewer Whig and more Tory M.P.s, as Charles had planned.

CHAPTER VII

DEFENDING THE CHARTER 1684—1725

As Charles II's marriage was childless, his brother James was heir to the throne. James had been brought up as a Protestant, but by 1671 he is thought to have been admitted to the Roman Church, though he continued to attend Anglican services until 1676. His two daughters, Mary and Anne, were brought up as Anglicans, but their mother became a Roman Catholic before her death, which was followed two years later by James marrying Mary of Modena, a Catholic. As we have seen, Charles had trouble with his parliaments, and ruled without one for many years while he re-arranged the charters of some boroughs to ensure a majority of Tories in parliament. The election of May 1685, the first one after this reorganisation, gave the new King James a parliament with a Tory majority, one which gave him the annual revenues that Charles had had, and £400,000 besides.

The efficient suppression of the Monmouth Rebellion and the harsh sentences of Judge Jeffreys in the resulting " Bloody Assizes " made James feel stronger than he really was. He kept a standing army of 20,000 men, and Roman Catholics were given commissions in it, despite the Test Act, which was designed to exclude from public office, those not of the established religion. Roman Catholics who would have been excluded by this Act were made privy councillors, and the leading Anglicans were driven from office. James wanted a parliament which would repeal all laws against the Catholics, and pass the Declaration of Indulgence. To ensure this, the borough corporations were put under pressure to remove those who would not conform.

During the Commonwealth, people in public office had been obliged to take the extreme, anti-Catholic Oath of the Solemn League and Covenant. In James' reign, and for some time afterwards these people were under pressure to repudiate this Oath. On Folio 26 of the borough records, there is a record of the election of Edward Purcell as mayor on the 4th of October, 1686. On the facing page is this statement:—

" Edward Purcell, Mayor of the Loyale Borrough and parish of Buckingham do declare that I hold that there was no obligation upon me or any other person from the Oath commonly called the Solemn League and Covenant; and that the same was in itself an Unlawful Oath and Imposed upon the subjects of this Realm against the known Laws and liberties of the Kingdom ".

The pressure was being put on the mayor to conform to the king's beliefs, and to supply members of parliament who would also conform.

In 1687 Jonathan Seyton was elected mayor in place of Edward Purcell, and in the same year two resignations took place. Sir Richard Temple resigned the office of steward, and J. Hugh Etherfoy resigned as alderman.

Jonathan Seyton must have resisted the political pressures of his king, as he was removed from office by His Majesty by an Order in Council, and replaced by Mr. George Dancer, who seems to have been equally obstinate in defying his king. Folio 30 states that he was removed from office by His Majesty and Thomas Shene elected in his place. On the facing page we can read that Thomas Shene suffered the same removal from office by an Order in Council, being replaced by Nathaniel Kent. It may be significant that none of these mayors appear to have repudiated the Oath of the Solemn League and Covenant.

The troubles were not yet over, as on Folio 32 there is a statement that the corporation was raising a mortgage for £100 for the defence of the charter. It seems that some money had already been raised, but more was needed, and was being raised, ' upon ye same security '. Despite all the efforts of the mayor and aldermen, the charter was surrendered. Later there was a proclamation for restoring surrendered charters, and Folio 34 records that the bailiff and burgesses of the ' Burrough and Parish of Buckingham ' were restored to their former rights and privileges. The Queen Mary Charter of 1554 was resumed and was in operation until 1835.

The town showed a further defiance of the king when a huge bonfire was lit here to celebrate the acquittal on June 30th, 1688 of the seven bishops who had been prosecuted by James for seditious libel. By the end of the year James had fled to France, to be replaced on the throne by his daughter Mary and her husband, William of Orange.

The Duke of Buckingham

George Villiers, Second Duke of Buckingham of the Villiers line, remained in retirement in the reign of James II, as he was not on good terms with the king. In early 1687 he caught a chill while hunting, and died at Kirby Moorside in the house of one of his tenants. As he was childless, his title died with him.

In 1703 John Sheffield, Marquess of Normanby, was created Duke of the County of Buckingham and Normanby. Lipscomb says that ' in order that he might not be considered (as it has been stated) an alien in the County, His Grace deemed it expedient to purchase a small estate in the Parish of Buckingham '. John Sheffield had served with the fleet in Charles II's reign, in the Dutch war, and had been in command of the fleet which was sent to defend Tangier. He died in 1723, when his son, Edmund succeeded him as Duke of Buckinghamshire and Normanby. The title became extinct in 1735 when Edmund died.

Expansion at Stowe[1]

Sir Richard Temple sat for Buckingham in the Restoration parliament of Charles II. He was an active member, helping the prosecution of those involved in the Popish Plot, and supporting the exclusion of James from the succession to the throne. As Steward of Buckingham he resigned in 1687, but was re-elected when the borough reverted to the Mary Charter.

When he died in 1697, the estate went to a second Sir Richard Temple, who had probably already served as a gentleman volunteer in the army in Flanders. Later he became the colonel of an infantry regiment, in which he found work for the Vicar of Stowe, the steward of the London household of the Temples, and his young brother Henry. In 1708 he took the despatch from Marlborough to Queen Anne, announcing the fall of Lille, an honour given him by the Duke of Marlborough. He was a brilliant soldier, and after the war became a Field-Marshal and received many other honours. His title, Baron and Viscount Cobham was used in the naming of the coaching inn, the Cobham Arms in West Street.

His military commands and a wealthy marriage brought him a fortune which was largely spent on improving the grounds of Stowe. Vanbrugh, the architect, and Bridgeman, who had designed the Serpentine and Kensington Gardens were employed to arrange the gardens, which were less formal than was usual at that time. Capability Brown worked at Stowe as an under-gardener, and later as head gardener. The spreading informality of his gardens would give pleasure to Lord Cobham but not to everyone, if there is any truth in the story that the village of Stowe was demolished in 1713, and the people moved to Dadford, to make room for the developments. The village may have disappeared earlier, however.

The church authorities would not be moved, and the village church remained near the house.

A Debtor at Bourton[2]

Sir Richard Minshull, the Royalist, lived at Bourton until his death in 1667, when his son Richard succeeded him. On this Richard's death in 1684, a third Richard Minshull lived at Bourton. This Richard Minshull was extravagant and led quite a splendid life. By 1692 he was in arrears over the tithes of Bourton and by 1699-1700 he probably mortgaged the manor, which went to Charles Vallop and others.

Richard Minshull was imprisoned in 1712 as a debtor in the King's Bench, and died there on the 17th of January, 1729-30. It has not been ascertained whether he stayed in prison for 17 years, or if he had a second imprisonment.

[1] The Stoic. National Dictionary of Biography.
[2] V.C.H. Bucks III, page 482. Sheahan page 248. Lipscomb II, page 588. Browne Willis pages 30, 32.

A Historian at Lenborough[3]

When Mr. William Robinson died in 1693, his relation, William Robinson sold the manor to Mr. John Rogers of Buckingham. This gentleman bought the titular manor—the lordship—from John Dormer, thus bringing into his own hands both the land and the lordship. This may have been social climbing or a good business move, to increase the value of his estate, which was bought in 1718 by Edward Gibbon, who moved into the manor house. His son, Edward Gibbon, the historian, was Lord of the Manor of Lenborough in 1735; in his time part of the house was taken down, the remainder being converted into a house for a tenant.

At Gawcott, Edmund Denton succeeded his father, Alexander, in 1698, and became a baronet the following year. The estate, along with Hillesden, passed by marriage to the Coke family.

Buildings of Buckingham[4]

Castle House passed out of Sir Edward Bagot's hands in 1667 when he and his wife, formerly May Lambert, sold it to Stephen Monteage of London. It was bought in 1680 by John Rogers of Buckingham, most probably the person who had bought Lenborough Manor. His son John, was Sheriff of Bucks in 1697, and an alderman and bailiff of Buckingham in 1718. The house was altered by his son, Matthias about 1708 or 1735, the front rooms rebuilt and 'made fit for the reception and accommodation of the Justices Itinerant, on their circuit'.

The Royal Latin School[5] was passing through a bad patch just after the town was granted its second charter. A house formerly used by the Chantry Priest stood next to the school, and at this time was used as a residence for the schoolmaster. This house was destroyed by fire in 1685, but the school seems to have escaped damage. Roundell tells the story that the schoolhouse was occupied by the widow and daughter of the previous master, Mr. Griffiths. The master at that time was Mr. Dalby, who was visiting Miss Mary Griffiths, spending the evening at the schoolhouse. The young couple were too busy to notice the fire till it was too late to extinguish the flames.

Three years later, possibly at the time that the corporation were fighting to defend their charter, the boys of the School went on a rampage against Popery, the religion of King James II, who was trying to deprive the town of its rights.

Browne Willis describes the school at this time in this way: ' Over the altar, on the boards of the ceiling, was depicted an holy lamb bleeding, and on each side two angels or monks, with cups to catch the blood. Underneath the lamb was St. John Baptist's

[3] V.C.H. Bucks III, page 484. Sheahan page 251. Lipscomb II, page 593.
[4] Lipscomb II, page 570. Harrison page 76.
[5] Harrison page 60. Roundell page 8.

head in a charger, and Ruding's motto, Alle may God amende; which was remaining till 1688, when it was destroyed as a relict of Popery by the schoolboys. The rest of the work was decorated with crescents and escallops, as were the panes of the windows and the back of the master's seat, being Ruding's arms, as in Buckingham chancel windows '.

The master's house was rebuilt in 1690, paid for by Alexander Denton. This house is still standing, but is now owned separately from the school.

Buckingham Churches and Chapels[6]

Sheahan says that at Gawcott there was at one time an ' Ancient Chapel dedicated to St. Catherine, the site of which is supposed to be a field called Chapel Close. The lane leading to it bears the name Chapel Lane. No remains of this place of worship existed in Browne Willis's time '.

In Buckingham a chapel was built in 1700 on the site of the present Congregational Church, not far from the place where two years earlier, the parish church had suffered its first, unexpected crash. On the 7th of February, 1698 the beautiful and much admired spire of the parish church had fallen to the ground, damaging the tower which supported it. The spire had been covered with lead, and probably the supporting wood had been weakened by rot and insects. Lipscomb says that the spire was blown down, and certainly the winds can blow hard in February. The damage was ' stated to exceed £1,000 '. It is surprising that after showing such spirit in opposing King James, the bailiff and burgesses seem to have made little or no attempt to rebuild their beloved spire. They seem to have received no help from the local boy of Bourton who had made good to the extent of becoming Lord Mayor of London[7].

This was Sir John Fleet, a person of ' humble parentage ' who had been apprenticed with the help of charity money, and worked his way up. Browne Willis said of him, ' I should pass him by as he was so destitute of gratitude, as not to contribute the least Charity to his native Parish in any of its greatest exigencies '. The fall of the spire must have been one of these exigencies, a calamity of the highest order—noisy, dusty and earth-shaking.

The task of raising money for this repair, as for so many other church buildings, was left to Browne Willis.

Browne Willis's[8] family had come to Buckinghamshire in 1675, when George Villiers was selling his estates in order to pay his debts. Browne Willis's grandfather, Dr. Thomas Willis bought some Villiers estates in Bletchley, Fenny Stratford and Water Eaton, and his son, Thomas Willis, in 1698, shared in the buying

[6] Lipscomb II, page 577.   Sheahan page 236.   Browne Willis page 82.
[7] Browne Willis page 40.   Sheahan page 246.
[8] Dragon of Whaddon by J. G. Jenkins.

of the Manor of Whaddon and Nash, Giffards Manor, Whaddon Chase, the park and the site of Snelshall Priory. At this time, the 16 years old Browne Willis was being educated at Westminster School, after a start at Beachampton School. His father's death in 1699 quickly followed by his mother's in 1700, was said by his brother to have brought on Browne Willis the ' falling sickness ' or epilepsy. He left Westminster, but soon went to Oxford University staying till 1704, when he left without taking a degree.

Browne Willis's short political life began in 1705, when he stood for Buckingham as a High Church Tory Member of Parliament. His opponent was Captain Tyrrell, who had left his regiment in Flanders to fight the seat. Captain Tyrrell was supported by Lord Wharton, but Browne Willis seems to have been supported by the townsfolk. The electorate consisted of the bailiff and twelve burgesses, which meant that seven votes were needed to win. When the poll was taken, Captain Tyrell had six votes and so had Browne Willis, ' upon which the mob, who were concerned to have a representative for the town, made diligent enquiry after the thirteenth person, who was missing, and at length found that he was in prison. After this, he was brought out, conducted to the market-place, where they took the votes, and being asked who he was for, resolutely declared he was for Mr. Willis '.

It is not certain where that prison stood, as our unique, castellated old gaol had not yet been built. Queen Mary's charter gave the right for a prison to be built in Buckingham, but whether this right was exercised is not known. Prisoners may have been held in the cellars of houses. The borough archivist suggests that Castle House may have been used.

Browne Willis did not seem to be bothered that his election depended on hauling a prisoner out of gaol, as he attended regularly at the House, but made no speeches. When parliament was dissolved in 1708 he was asked if he cared to stand again, but declined. Roundell says that ' though he retained his seat in Parliament only four years, he never ceased to be grateful for the honour conferred upon him '. He helped the town financially, and by continually referring to Buckingham as ' the County Town ' he tried to ensure that it would keep this position.

Browne Willis's love for Buckingham led him to write begging letters to his neighbours, for money for use in building and renovating the town. One letter to Alexander Denton, M.P. for Buckingham at that time, quoted in " The Dragon of Whaddon ", is charming and well-designed to open the Denton purse strings. Other letters written by Browne Willis were less charming, as he had other sides to his character than that of a supporter of Buckingham. Although he was friendly with the Verneys of Claydon, he was at odds with many of the other gentry of the district, including Lord Cobham of Stowe. They differed in politics, but both helped Buckingham in many ways.

Browne Willis's dislike of Lord Cobham did not prevent him writing a short poem as a very touching begging letter—begging for funds to rebuild Buckingham church spire.

> On Buckingham—depressed County Town,
> From Stowe's ennobled altitude look down;
> Worthy of being parent to a shire
> Let it by your munificence appear;
> That clamorous faction may no more upbraid
> Its humble dwellings, loss of friends and trade,
> There fix your Castle, there let Columns stand,
> Emblems of love raised by a grateful hand;
> Oh, look on it as first it looked on you,
> Exalt again its Spire to crown your view,
> And ancient Magisterial rights renew;
> All ages then the Patriot shall record,
> And sing, How suitable are thy Temples, Lord.

This poem was meant to appeal to the Lord of Stowe in a friendly way, but Willis must have spent many more hours writing other poems to Lord Cobham, poems which were as deliberately insulting as a clever man could make them.

The rectors of Bletchley were in a particularly vulnerable position as Browne Willis was patron of the living of Bletchley. He felt it his duty to supervise and criticise the incumbent as well as present him to the living. Uninvited and prolonged visits by Browne Willis were the fate of the rectors, which some accepted wearily, but others replied to with vigour, even bringing the battle into the pulpit. Two of his sons served as rectors of Bletchley, and relations with them were as strained as with the other rectors. With all his sons he seems to have expected continual gratitude for any help or gift, while they felt that their enthusiastic, energetic father was unreasonable and quarrelsome. Another cause of friction was their belief that he was a spendthrift in that he spent so much money on church buildings and historical enquiries.

These historical interests took him all over England, and gave him contacts with antiquarians from Oxford, Cambridge, and other places. Churches and their history was a major interest, but he also made important collections of coins and published many books. Among these is the " Antiquities of Buckingham ", a book to read with enjoyment and interest.

One rector of Bletchley shared Browne Willis's interest in history, which formed a friendly basis for their relationship. This was the Reverend William Cole, who was rector when Browne Willis died. Even this rector suffered somewhat from unexpected visits and demands that he should pay for repairs to the neglected rectory, but the friendship survived the quarrels, as there was a real respect for each other.

As he grew older, Willis seems to have become more eccentric.

His friend Cole describes him as, " more the appearance of a mumping beggar than of a gentleman; and the most like resemblance of his figure that I can recollect among old prints is that of Old Hobson the Cambridge carrier. He then, as always, was dressed in an old slouched hat, more brown than black, a weather-beaten large wig, three or four old-fashioned coats, all tied round by a leather belt, and over all an old blue cloak, lined with black fustian, which he told me he had new made when he was elected member for the town of Buckingham about 1707[9]. I have still by me, as relics, this cloak and belt which I purchased of his servant ".

Cole must have thought a great deal of his untidy friend to have bought his old clothes. In another place he says, " His boots, which he almost always appeared in, were not the least singular part of his dress. I suppose it will not be falsity to say they were forty years old, patched and vamped up at various times. They were all in wrinkles and don't come up above half way of his legs. He was often called in the neighbourhood Old Wrinkle Boots ".

The coach that Willis used did not escape his friend's attention, " The chariot of Mr. Willis was so singular that from it he was called himself, The Old Chariot. It was his wedding chariot, and had his arms on brass plates about it, not unlike a coffin and painted black ".

The coat of arms was dear to Browne Willis, as he had taken great pains to deduce his descent and that of his wife, from Walter Giffard, Earl of Buckingham, though when in a bad temper he would tell his son Thomas that his family came from nothing.

Despite his quarrels and eccentricities, he was a steadfast friend to Buckingham as is shown by his actions and his writings, and the way he pushed and persuaded his friends into helping the town. " And it would no less redound to the Glory of the Gentry of the Shire, to which it gives Name; if they also would unite in their Endeavours, to improve and adorn it in such a Manner, as to render it in all Respects fit to be esteemed The Capital of a County ".

[9] Browne Willis was elected M.P. for Buckingham in 1705.

CHAPTER VIII

THE FIRE AT BUCKINGHAM 1725

THE evening of March 15th, 1725 was fine and dry, as it had been for some days. It was good March weather, and a brisk wind blew around the streets. Castle Street looked different from today, and amongst its old buildings was a hostelry called the Unicorn Inn. Near this inn was a yard owned by Mr. Henderson[1], where a maid and two boys were playing about. Somehow a light was dropped onto a stack of furze, which quickly started to burn, the flames being fanned by the wind.

The neighbours would run with buckets of water to try to put out the fire, and people from the Unicorn would help too, but in those days there were only the most primitive means of fighting fires, which therefore could be much more destructive than they usually are today.

The fire spread quickly, passing along the roofs and dry wood-work of the houses, blazing up at stables containing hay for feed and straw for bedding. The direction of the wind is not known, but most of Castle Street was burnt, then the fire spread round Castle Hill, destroying the houses on the hill towards Tingewick Bridge. Market Hill to the north of the start of the fire was also affected, as houses were burnt as far as the present Hilton's shoe shop, which was alight but was not destroyed. The fire spread beyond the other side of Castle Street, so that part of Bourtonhold, Well Street and West Street were burnt.

The church with its fallen spire was untouched, as was the manor house, the vicarage, Trinity House, Castle House and, surprisingly, the old Town Hall. Other buildings near the Town Hall were burnt, as is shown by the charred timbers recently found in Railton's shoe shop in Castle Street, when some structural alterations were being done.

The fire was reported in a London newspaper in this way[2], " On Monday last, the 15th of the Instant March, about seven in the Evening, a dreadful Fire broke out near the Unicorn Inn in Buckingham; which burnt with such Vehemency, that it soon consumed 138 Dwelling Houses, besides Out-houses, Barns, Stables, Hay, Corn, etc. By which Defoliation above 200 families are miserably undone; and it is computed that the Loss cannot amount to less than £40,000 there being very few that had the least Opportunity of saving their Goods ".

As there were 387 houses in Buckingham at that time, more than one third of the houses were destroyed, and more than one

---

[1] Roundell page 28.
[2] Browne Willis page 28.

third of the people would be homeless. As houses in normal times were often small and overcrowded, this fire would mean even more people being accommodated in the cottages and houses that were left intact. People living in North End would help their friends in the centre of the town, who had lost their houses, and neighbours would take in a family or a few children. Some would not be able to move in with another family, and would manage with a cellar of the burnt-out shells of their ruined houses.

In those days, as now, appeals were made for money to help the victims of such disasters, and the " Northampton Mercury " of 22nd March, 1725, gives a warning concerning the collection of money, " . . . . And whereas on such dreadful Accidents several idle and loose persons do, without any lawful Authority, go begging about the country, under false Pretences of Losses by such Fires. Therefore, to prevent such ill Practices, These are, in the Names of all the Inhabitants of the said town, to give Notice, that whensoever an Application shall be made to any Place for their charity, it will be done by Persons of the said Town, who are of good Reputation, and shall have due Authority for that Purpose ".

The Persons of Good Reputation with due Authority must have been busy, and the surrounding towns reacted generously to the news of Buckingham's fire. The " Northampton Mercury " reported, " We hear that the Town of Aylesbury collected and sent the very next day to the poor sufferers 53 gns."

Harrison reports another contribution, " April 1725, Collected at Wendover for a fire at Buckingham, £25 14s. 6d.—the largest collection ever known at Wendover ".

Insurance covered some of the damage, but Harrison says that " the loss over and above all money recovered from any insurance office whatsoever amounted to £32,682 13s. 6d." which would be a catastrophic amount for as small a town as Buckingham. It was probably fortunate that the Sun Insurance Company opened an office in Buckingham on the 17th May, 1721, with William Cooper as the agent. This agency, which is still doing business, would probably deal with claims for the 1725 fire.

The neighbouring towns and villages helped Buckingham generously, but the corporation was not as enterprising in rebuild-the town as might have been expected, especially considering how strongly they had reacted to King James II's interference with their affairs. The Victoria History reports that some people were pulling down large houses in order to sell the materials to build small houses, which would hardly be a paying business unless the cost of building materials had risen sharply because of the fire.

This was the very opposite to what Browne Willis hoped would happen. He was indignant that the fire was not looked on as an opportunity to improve Buckingham by replacing the burnt buildings with better new ones. In 1730 he described his reactions to the fire in his " Notitia Parliamentaria " and he quotes from this in his "Antiquities of Buckingham"[3]. He said that the fire was a great misfortune, but it might have been used to produce a better town than before. This could have been done by obtaining an Act of Parliament as had happened at Northampton and Warwick, and would have helped in the rebuilding of the town. As this Act had not been obtained, it "tended greatly towards impoverishing the Town, and sunk its Trade and Markets, which it is to be feared will decay more and more". By 1730, he says, not even a third of the burnt houses had been rebuilt, "and those that have been begun are not carried up in any uniformity; there not being any attempt towards setting out the Streets, the Omission of which must always be regretted by such who cannot but have at Heart the Credit and Interest of this their Mother-Town in particular, or future Reputation of the County in general". Some people must have been making the best of a bad situation by saying that in the end, they would have "handsome and convenient Dwellings" in place of the "bad or indifferent Houses" that they had before the fire. Browne Willis thought otherwise, "yet it will I fear, turn out quite otherwise in the end; and that the Damage will at length exceed the highest Calculation, must be apparent to all such who are conversant in Trade; for it is not the Quality or Fineness of Building, but Quantity of Offices, and Rooms for Conveniency, that furnish out Necessaries for Shopkeepers; and if these are not provided for in Time, there can be little Reparation in erecting them, after the Trade is irretrievably gone hence, and transplanted elsewhere".

In this confused and depressing situation, one person was making an effort to rehouse the poorer people. This was Willis's adversary, Lord Cobham of Stowe, who built some "high brick houses" called the Red Buildings in North End at the site of the cattle market. These were not pretty, but were very useful at the time, and remained there until 1866 when they deteriorated and were condemned and demolished.

Browne Willis attributes the decrease in the prosperity of the town to the fire, and the slowness in rebuilding afterwards. Many other people have agreed with him and felt that the fire marked a turning point in the life of Buckingham.

[3] Browne Willis page 29.

CHAPTER IX

THE NEW GAOL 1725—1760

In 1735 Browne Willis wrote his book entitled " The History and Antiquities of the Town, Hundred, and Deanery of Buckingham ". In this book is the history of the town up to that date; the facts are interspersed with comments. Much of Browne Willis's thoughts seem to have been on the status of Buckingham; whether the assizes were held here, and whether in the eyes of the rest of the county, Buckingham was the county town. He also took a great interest in the state of the castle, and deplored that it had been allowed to fall into ruins.

He thought that the castle had at one time been reduced to a farm-house, basing this belief on a grant made by Queen Elizabeth in 1574 to Edward Grimston of " the Castle Farm in Buckingham, and two Mills called Castle Mills ". He may have been correct, or Castle Farm may have been even then, a farm that was not actually on Castle Hill.

In 1735 the houses on Castle Hill that had been burnt by the fire, had not yet been rebuilt, and the castle had been reduced to " a dark Room or two on the North Corner of the Hill, next Castle Street, inhabited by poor People, which overlooks the Town, and is seen above the rest of the Houses; which Part, as I conceive, was left standing because it had been antiently used as a Chapel to the Prison, it being called Chapel-End ".[1] Buckingham Castle had been used as a prison in 1534-5[2], but it must have ceased to be used in that way for some time before Browne Willis was alive.

Some other building was used as a gaol in 1743 to hold Mr. Sansbury, who had been tried at the Summer Assizes at Buckingham for robbing a tax collector on Whitchurch Hill, and was found guilty. According to Silvester he belonged to a gang of robbers, " footmen ", who waylaid travellers. Robbing a tax collector was a serious offence, and Mr. Sansbury would leave the court room knowing that he would play the main part in a public execution. During the night a shot was fired, and the authorities, fearing a rescue attempt, executed him the following day. This was the last public execution at Buckingham. Gallows Hill is where Western Avenue meets Moreton Road, and the Gallows Tree is probably the large, old tree beside Overn Hill House, almost on the corner of Western Avenue. Probably Mr. Sansbury would be brought up Moreton Road, then called Podds Lane, and would be hung on the gallows till dead, then left to swing as a warning to others— beware of the tax collectors !

[1] Browne Willis page 50.
[2] V.C.H. Bucks IV page 525.

Silvester, writing in the 1850's gives an interesting alternative for the siting of the gallows. He says, " The gallows formerly stood where Mrs. Bartlett's house now stands, and some years before it was taken down, it used to be stored in Tunk's garden ". As far as can be ascertained, the Bartlett's house was in Hunter Street, very near the old parish church, which was then in use. This would hardly be a suitable place for a gallows, which were usually put in a prominent position, either in the town or on a road leading to the town.

The rivalry between Buckingham and Aylesbury for position as County Town, continued for many years. In 1572 an Act was passed for keeping the assizes at Aylesbury, but Buckingham had not given up the contest. There appears to be some doubt as to when the summer assizes were resumed at Buckingham, but in the second half of the 17th century, Thomas Baskerville had said that the assizes were held in sheds erected against the ruined walls of Buckingham Castle. As well as giving Thomas Baskerville's observations, the Victoria History says on another page that from 1720 onwards the summer assizes were held here[3]. Mr. Jenkins, writing about this subject in " The Dragon of Whaddon "[4] says that Browne Willis arranged for the assizes to be held here from 1724-1728. At any rate it seems certain that despite the Act of 1572 the summer assizes were, as a matter of convenience, resumed at Buckingham some time later. The Victoria History says that Aylesbury protested that not only was Buckingham inconveniently situated, but that it had no gaol, as the one for the county was at Aylesbury. However, there must have been some sort of a lock-up here, as prisoners would have to be held here for the summer assizes, and the unfortunate Mr. Sansbury was tried one day here, and executed the next day. It seems unlikely that he would have been taken to Aylesbury to stay the night, then brought back to Buckingham to be executed; the chance of rescue as he travelled along the road would be too great.

Browne Willis wanted Buckingham to be recognised as the place where the assizes were held—by right, and not by favour or chance. He worked for this, and would rejoice with the rest of the town when in 1748 an Act of Parliament was obtained by which the summer assizes were fixed here. The fact that the Act was passed by the influence of Browne Willis's enemy, Lord Cobham, would not make " Old Wrinkle Boots " any happier, but I am sure that his love for Buckingham was greater than his dislike of the owner of Stowe.

The lack of a suitable gaol at Buckingham had been in Willis's mind for many years. In 1743 Lord Fermanagh of Claydon wrote to his father and reported that Willis had been dining at Claydon

[3] V.C.H. Bucks IV, page 548.
[4] Dragon of Whaddon by J. G. Jenkins, page 112.

and was begging for £140 in order to build Buckingham gaol[5]. We are not told whether anyone from Claydon House contributed towards the project, but it is generally stated in books of the district that the gaol was built in 1748 at the expense of Lord Cobham. Harrison quotes a memorial stone that in his day was in the north wall of the gaol, and even then was hardly decipherable. According to Harrison, this stone gave 1758 as the year in which the gaol was erected.

When built, the gaol was square, and did not have the semi-circular residence on the market side, which was added in 1839. The gaol now has an inner courtyard, an exercise yard, with a high wall on the sides facing North End and Clay's shop. The side facing the market has the former superintendent's residence, and the side facing the King's Head, which contained the cells, now has the lower cells incorporated in a restaurant, but four of the six upper ones are in almost their original condition, each with a small window overlooking the courtyard, and an inner and outer door, each with a peep-hole covered with mesh wire.

The gaol, though impressive and strongly built, was soon almost empty. Silvester says, " The gaol for Buckingham had no water, and the gaoler no salary, nor had he at this time any prisoners except a raving lunatic ". His account of the gaol was taken from the Appendix to State Prisons 1st edition, page 134, and he thought that the gaol had been visited about 1780.

Harrison tells of an escape by " Scroggs " Wesley, who made himself a noose rope of blanket shreds, which he threw over the battlements. He then climbed up the wall on the inside of the gaol, and then slid down the rope on the outside. One prisoner, the " Coiner " Varney, walked out when he had an opportunity, as did another prisoner who afterwards hid in the cemetery plantation while the police searched for him miles away.

Buckingham benefited from the kindness of Lord Cobham of Stowe[6]. He built the Red Buildings after the fire, and he arranged for the assizes to be held at Buckingham by right, as well as his most lasting and spectacular gift—the gaol. Other stories about him are not so complimentary and possibly not true, as it is said that two local men went poaching in his deer park, and when they did not return home, their wives went to the great Lord Cobham to ask and beg for their husbands to be returned to them. Their wish was granted, and their husbands were brought home—dead, as they had been hanged at the personal order of the master of Stowe. He is said to have celebrated the event by erecting their statues in one of his garden walks. This is a colourful story, but possibly mere legend.

[5] Dragon of Whaddon by J. G. Jenkins, page 113.
[6] The Stoic, Volume XXIII, Number 3, July 1968. The History of Stowe V.

With his success as a soldier, and his success in marrying a wealthy heiress, Lord Cobham had the means to rebuild Stowe House and arrange new, bigger and no doubt, better gardens. He had a wonderful property to leave to his heir, but unfortunately he had no children. His heir was his second cousin, William Temple, who was not of the same calibre as himself. This young man was said to be of " dubious character ". To quote from " The Stoic ", ' Even his mother seems to have distrusted him, for she made his brother and sister executors of her will and left him £300 on the condition that they found him " worthy and deserving of it ". His uncle, Sir Purbeck Temple, was more outspoken, " William Temple (altho' he be my heir at Law) shall have noe part or benefit of my estate real or personal whatsoever, except the Legacy of 1s." —the proverbial shilling.

Lord Cobham was kinder than this in his treatment of his heir. He offered William a choice, either he could receive £7,000 (equivalent to £100,000 in modern terms) in return for signing away his rights and those of his successors, to the Stowe property, or he could retain his rights and hope that the 41 years old Lord Cobham would die childless. William chose to take the £7,000, and Lord Cobham was free to leave his property to whoever he wished. He arranged that his property and title would pass to his sister Hester and her heir, and if that line failed, to his next sister, Lady Lyttelton and her heir. These arrangements were made by 1718, and Lord Cobham would still hope that he would have a male child of his own to succeed him. When he died in 1749 he was still childless, and his forethought in dealing with his property was shown to be worthwhile. His sister Hester, became Countess Temple and inherited Stowe, bringing her husband Richard Grenville and her politically active sons to the house.

Hester's son, Richard Grenville succeeded to the estate in 1752, a wealthy man, interested in politics, active, but not as intelligent as his younger brother George, who became Prime Minister. This family of Grenvilles had a great influence on the direction of the affairs of England. The two brothers helped the elder Pitt to oppose Walpole, then Pitt married Hester Grenville, sister of Richard and George. Stowe became a place where political meetings took place—meetings of brothers and brothers-in-law. In 1756 Richard Temple, Earl Temple, became First Lord of the Admiralty, probably because his sister had married Pitt. Later he was Lord Privy Seal, and a lone supporter of Pitt in his proposal to declare war on Spain. Still later he supported John Wilkes instead of Pitt, then left politics to live at Stowe.

Browne Willis had not been idle during these years. He had been continually concerned in the repair of the church. In 1737 he had written to Mr. Justice Denton[7] informing him that " a

---

[7] The Church Bells of Buckinghamshire by A. H. Cocks, M.A., page 330.

superstructure " was to be " erected on the present Tower, after taking down the monstrous Balcony ". The unfinished look of the church concerned him, and also the behaviour of the bell ringers, as he continues, " and the Bells mounted and then the ropes may no longer dangle indecently in the Church or Ale carried to be drunk in the middle of it and other Acts done which breed and instill into youth Future irreverence to the place ". Apparently bell ringers needed their ale, but Browne Willis would rather they were not seen drinking it.

His continual begging for money to repair the spire did produce results. In 1753 he wrote to the Master of Magdalene College, Cambridge, telling him that[8], " I have been making a very elegant Tower Steeple by taking down the most deformed irregular top of what was built up after the fall of the lofty spire about 52 years ago and relating it to the model of the rest of the fabric, and raising it about 30 feet. So that it is now by far the handsomest and highest tower in the county and seen some miles round about, and sets off the town and makes it again appear and show itself with dignity". He says that it is costing more than he expected, and he seems to have put a great deal of his own money into the project.

His feelings two years later had changed, as in his " Antiquities of Buckingham " published in 1755, he writes about the tower, " the top Part was pulled down, and made up with small, irregular, mean Pinacles, Pediments, and Ballisters, most improperly placed round it, and so left, carried up only a little higher than the old Tower, in no Order or Style of Architecture corrrespondent to any other Parts of the Fabrick ". He says that considerable sums of money had been contributed towards the repairs, the two members of parliament for the town giving £100 each, and two knights of the shire 20 guineas each, as well as other contributions. The lead and timber from the old spire had been sold to help with the cost, but Browne Willis was not satisfied with the result.

His book, " The Antiquities of Buckingham " contained information, much of which had been obtained at his own expense. He employed a man to copy documents for him, copying entries in registers, old wills and other papers. Willis travelled throughout the country for information, and in the opinion of his family, spent more than was wise on his enquiries.

In working for the improvement in the status of Buckingham, he tried for many years to arrange that the Bishop of Lincoln should hold his episcopal visitation here. In February 1756 he wrote to Lord Verney asking his help to arrange this[5], " As your Lordship is so near the Bishop of Lincoln, who has a house in Albemarle Street, I most earnestly and importunately wish your Lordship

[8] Dragon of Whaddon by J. G. Jenkins, page 109.
[5] Dragon of Whaddon by J. G. Jenkins, page 113.

would engage him to hold his Triennial Visitation at poor Buckingham. It might be as good as an Assize to the town and I would, if it cost me half a score of pounds, see that his lordship and the clergy should be nobly accommodated. Indifferent the Lord High Steward and Alderman Murgetty will be about it, especially if they know I endeavor it ".

Browne Willis seems to be once again at odds with other people connected with the town, but he had his wish, and the Bishop of Lincoln did come to Buckingham. Willis told his friend the Rev. Cole that the bishop's first visit had been four years earlier.

At this time Buckingham was not an isolated town, as coach services that had started in the previous century, were still continuing. This is shown by a letter from Henry Purefoy to Peter Moulson written in August 1753. The letter says that the Birmingham Coach runs through in a day from London to Buckingham, the fare being ten shillings per passenger. The passengers would be dropped at the inn formerly called the Cobham Arms, and later changed to the Earl Temple's Arms. Henry Purefoy made his own arrangements for his guest, as he says, " If you will let us know when you will come, our chariot shall meet you at Buckingham ".

Mr. Harrison on page 94 quotes a placard about the coach service in 1779. It reads: " The Banbury, Buckingham and Winslow machine begins going for the winter season on Saturday, 20th November, 1779".

" Sets out from the ' Red Lion ' Inn, in Banbury, every Saturday, Tuesday and Thursday, at noon, to Buckingham; and returns from there every Sunday, Wednesday, and Friday morning. Likewise a coach from the ' Cobham Arms ', Buckingham every Sunday, Wednesday and Friday morning at five o'clock to London; and return from there every Tuesday, Thursday and Saturday morning to Buckingham, at the same hour. The fare as usual. Inside passengers to be allowed 14 lb. for luggage; all above to pay one penny per pound. Performed by John Lomax and Co. Stops at the ' Plough ' at Adderbury, ' Red Lion ' at Aynho, ' Barley Mow ' on Baynard's Green, ' White Hart ' at Buckingham, and ' The Three Pigeons ' at Winslow, to take up and set down passengers and parcels. Stops going in and coming out of London at the ' Green Man and Still ', the corner of Swallow Street, Oxford Road ".

The guests of the Grenvilles would make use of the coach service, and when driving to Stowe from Buckingham would be duly impressed as they came to the Corinthian Arch, which so efficiently belittles the visitor, and magnifies the importance of the owner of Stowe house beyond.

1760 was a year in which a number of things happened which were of interest to the people of Buckingham. In that year, Lord Temple became a Knight of the Garter, a great honour then, as now. A Mr. Gabriel Newton, Alderman of the borough of Leicester, by an Indenture dated March 15th, 1760, gave "certain estates in trust to the Corporation of Leicester and their successors, that they should, out of the rents and profits of the same, pay yearly to several mayors, etc., of various places, several sums of money for clothing, schooling, and educating a certain number of boys of indigent and necessitous parents of the established Church of England. Amongst others the Corporation of Buckingham was left the yearly sum of £26 for clothing etc., 25 boys of the before-mentioned description "[9]. By 1862 these boys were being educated at the National School in School Lane.

On the 5th February, 1760 Browne Willis died[10]. Mr. John Gibberd, curate of Whaddon gives a sincere and kind picture of Willis's last moments, " During this last year he gave me repeated assurances, without any solicitation, of using his interest and good offices with the Archbishop of Canterbury in my behalf; and he breathed almost his last with the most earnest and ardent wishes for my prosperity: ' Ah, Mr. Gibberd, God bless you for ever, Mr. Gibberd ! ' were almost the last words of my dying friend ".

Mr. Cole reports a death scene with a touch of the old Browne Willis showing even at the end. He says that " when Mr. Cook of Water Eaton, Browne Willis's steward came into the dying man's room, the squire passionately demanded a small sum of money which the steward owed him ". The debt was later paid to Willis's grandson.

Browne Willis had wished that only the Mayor and Aldermen, or Bailiff and Burgesses of Buckingham should attend his funeral, and on the 11th February, 1760, six aldermen were present and each received a gift of six shillings and eight pence and a copy of the first volume of the ' Notitia Parliamentaria ' which may be a sign of the value that Browne Willis placed on his association with Buckingham.

[9] Sheahan page 242.
[10] Dragon of Whaddon by J. G. Jenkins, page 213.

CHAPTER X

A REFORMED CORPORATION 1760—1835

A PLAN of the town of Buckingham was produced in 1770, surveyed and engraved by Thomas Jeffreys[1]. At that time the town was still contained within the curve of the river and was little changed compared with John Speed's plan of 1610. The small group of houses in what is now Mitre Street and Lenborough Road, had not significantly altered, but a road through the fields joined Gawcott Road to Tingewick Road, continuing the shorter path seen in Speed's plan. This is Bath Lane, though it is not named in Jeffrey's plan.

The church was still standing, spireless, in the old churchyard, with a fulling mill down Mill Lane, at the riverside nearby. The Manor House, Vicarage and Trinity House were there, but the street on which they stand was called St. Rumbald's Lane, not Church Street as now. The Castle Mills stood at the corner of Nelson Street and Tingewick Road, on the site of the paint factory, with the bare Castle Hill above it. Nelson Street was then called Bristle Hill (in 1770 Nelson was a boy of 12, who had just been entered in the " Raisonnable " with his uncle, Captain Suckling). Beyond Castle Hill there was a large tree, the Cutterne Elm, which has since been chopped down. This famous tree gave its name to Elm Street, which in 1770 was called Hog Lane. The significance of the names Hog Lane and Bristle Hill has not been ascertained.

By 1770 Well Street and Castle Street seem to have been almost completely rebuilt, thus filling the gaps created by the fire in 1725. The old town hall, later demolished in 1783, stood in the centre of the town, in front of the White Hart, and the present town hall was yet to be built. The Old Latin School was labelled ' Chapel ', and the groups of buildings on either side of the Chewar were clearly drawn. The group of buildings now including Wetherhead's shop was then standing in the High Street, which Sir Nikolaus Pevsner calls " a most successful island of two low cottages of even roofs ". Further along the High Street was the gaol, wrongly labelled as a castle. A few new buildings had sprung up along the entrance to Podds Lane, and a building which has since disappeared, was standing in the ' North East End '; possibly this was the Red Buildings erected after the fire.

Bridge Street was still an unimportant lane, with the London Road leaving Buckingham over the Sheriff's Bridge, and continuing between fields to Winslow. On the 1770 plan a few houses are shown where the Thornborough Road leaves the London Road

[1] V.C.H. Bucks III, pages 474-475.

outside the town, but these are the only houses on this road outside the town.

It would seem from this plan that Buckingham had not suffered permanently from the effects of the fire. Forty-five years after the fire the town appears to be as full of houses as it was in 1610; but the plan cannot show the state of the shops and small industries.

On March 26th, 1776 an earth-shaking event occurred in Buckingham. This is described in a letter in Mr. Harrison's collection of papers. The letter is written in 1878, by Mr. A. R. Carter of Oxford; writing about Buckingham, he says, " . . . My Grandfather, Richard Garrett who lies buried in his Father's grave, over which is a tombstone . . . . was born in 1764 and died in 1853 in his 89th year. When I was a boy I remember asking him if he had known the old church and recollected its falling down and he told me that he knew it well and recollected the sudden and unexpected fall of the Steeple. He had just come through the Churchyard and was on his way home through Church Street into Well Street . . . . and he had scarcely got to the turning into Well Street when he was startled by a sudden roar or explosion something like a prolonged peal of thunder, and the street was filled with a dense cloud of dust something like a thick fog. It occurred about 8.0 o'clock in the evening, and if I recollect aright he said the Curfew bell had just ceased. Of this however, I am not quite positive. I find on reference to the " Gentleman's Mag." that the Steeple of Buckingham Parish Church fell down on the 26th March, 1776, consequently my grandfather was then 12 years of age.

My Father doubts the curfew having rung on that night because it is the rule, dating from far back times, to suspend it from March 25th to September 29th but my impression still is that my Grandfather mentioned the fact I refer to which indeed seemed to me to explain the actual time of the fall as an immediate result of the vibrations ".

A. H. Cocks in his ' The Church Bells of Buckinghamshire ' says that ' The increased weight of the masonry added to the tower in 1753, proved too great for the old piers which supported it, and on March 26th, 1776, the tower fell, only a few minutes after the ringers had left it '.

When Mr. Cocks wrote his book in 1897, the curfew bell was still rung in Buckingham. Referring to the bells in the present parish church, he says, ' From Michaelmas Day to Lady Day, the fifth is rung for about five minutes, at 6 a.m. and the common tradition exists here, of a person who was lost, finding out his or her whereabouts on hearing a bell, and leaving money for this ringing to be continued in perpetuity through the dark half of the year. Rung again as the curfew at 8 p.m.; evidently a survival of the Morning and Evening Ave '. The ringing of the curfew bell ceased in 1940.

He tells us of other ringing customs in the town. On Shrove Tuesday the seventh was rung for about ten minutes as a Pancake Bell, some time between 10 a.m. and noon, usually from 11.50 to 12 noon, a custom which has recently been revived.

The Death Knell for persons over twelve years of age was on the tenor, under twelve on the second bell. " At the conclusion, after a minute's pause, nine strokes on the tenor for a male, and six for a female ".

He says that the sixth is said to be the Fire Bell. Neither the Passing Bell nor the Fire Bell are now rung.

According to Roundell[2], sometime after 1688 the Latin School once again became dilapidated. The roof fell in, the ground floor was dug up, and used by a neighbour as a vegetable garden. The garden and courtyard had been used as other things than a garden, as Harrison says that human remains have been found there, suggesting that it was at one time a cemetery. It is hard to see how the building could still be used as a school with no roof or floor, but there are no obvious gaps in the list of masters of the school at this time.

When the tower of the parish church fell in 1776, the whole building was in such a poor state that it was decided to pull down the entire building and start again. Some of the timber from the old church was used for a new roof for the Latin School, paid for by Earl Temple. Some oak pew[3] ends were also taken from the old church and used in the school.

As the town had no parish church, the school was used once again as a chapel, with half the congregation attending in the morning and the other half in the afternoons. Harrison says that at that time a gallery was erected round the sides of the building, and later an entire floor was laid across the room, supported on gallery pillars, so that the original building was divided into two rooms, the upper one being used as a school and the lower as a store or cellar. This floor has since been removed.

The town did not wait long for its new church. Earl Verney[4] gave the site on Castle Hill for a new church, Earl Temple undertook to build the church, with some of the material from the old building and money raised by bonds, one of which is shown in Harrison's book. He himself also contributed to the funds.

The first stone was laid by Robert Bartlett, Esq., on 25th November, 1777 and the building was consecrated by the Bishop of Lincoln on December 6th, 1781.

This was a time of church building in Buckingham, as in the following year, 1782, a Wesleyan chapel was built in Well Street. In the same year the bells for the parish church were made by

[2] Roundell page 8.
[3] Harrison page 60.
[4] Sheahan page 236.   Harrison page 48.   Lipscomb II, page 580.

Chapman and Mears of London, and were first rung on the 7th of March, 1783.

The church when built was quite different from now, as it had no chancel and no buttresses.

Lipscomb describes it as a " plain unornamented edifice of free stone ", but Lipscomb found it difficult to say anything nice about Buckingham. The church has a battlemented tower, with a handsome octagonal spire rising 150 feet from the ground. This spire is visible for many miles around, as the church is so prominently placed on Castle Hill. The interior of the church was quite different in 1783, with columns and a decorated plaster ceiling. The columns divided the church into three aisles, with a gallery on each side, supported by the columns. A picture in the Church Guide shows the semi-circular ceiling, a three-decker pulpit (part of which is now in Great Brickhill Church) and a chandelier, a gift from Browne Willis to the old parish church, and one of the few things to be brought to the new building. The communion-plate, the vestry chest and a benefaction board were also brought from the old church. The Marquis of Buckingham presented a copy of Raphael's ' Transfiguration ', and this was placed above the altar. The people of the town would be pleased with their new church, and would be able to leave the St. John the Baptist Chapel where services had been held.

Early in the 19th century further work was done on the parish church. Sheahan reports that in 1820 the gallery was erected at the west end of the church, being paid for by subscription. In this gallery there was an organ bearing this inscription, ' Georgius King, Londini, Fecit 1801. No. 24, Marsham Street, Westminster '. Sheahan says that by the will of Philip Box, Esq., dated 16th February, 1811, £1,000 was left to be invested by the Corporation to pay the salary of an organist.

In 1822 a large east window was erected[5] 'as a token of his affection and regard for the borough and its inhabitants ' by ' the Most High, Most Mighty, and Most Noble Prince Richard Duke of Buckingham and Chandos, Marquess of Chandos and Buckingham and Earl Temple of Stowe, Marquess of Buckingham, Earl Temple, and Viscount and Baron Cobham '.

In the year in which the church bells were first rung, the present town hall was built. Harrison on page 127 notes that ' 1783— The Corporation met at the ' Cobham Arms Inn ' as the old Sessions House was pulled down and the new Town Hall was not finished. (See Corporation Records, page 191) '.

Among Mr. Harrison's papers[6] there is a cutting referring to a theatre which he says was constructed over the coach houses of the ' Swan and Castle ' Hotel. The cutting says that a printed

5 Sheahan page 237.
6 Harrison page 30. Harrison's papers.

play-bill was preserved at Shalstone Manor House, relating to a performance in this theatre ' by desire of Mrs. Purefoy ' on the 22nd of December, 1790. This piece was a comic opera entitled ' Inkle and Yarico ' ; it was performed by Mr. Hounslow's Company of Comedians, with Mr. White and Miss Harvey in the name-parts. At the end of the play Mr. Young kindly danced a hornpipe and Mr. Henley performed something—perhaps a monologue—called ' The Greenwich Pensioner '. Finally there was a farce called ' The Romp '. The charges for this varied and lengthy entertainment were, boxes 3/-, the pit 2/- and the gallery 1/-.

Harrison says that about 1800 there was another building which was occasionally used as a theatre. This was a stone barn on the London Road, but it was pulled down even before 1909 when Harrison wrote his book[7].

Before Mr. Box's death in 1811 he had opened a bank in the town. This was in 1786[8]; notes were issued by the bank, made payable at the Banking House of Messrs Praed & Co., Fleet-Street, London. Mr. Box had been a draper, and served as Receiver-General of Taxes for Bucks., and in the Commission of the Peace.

New partners were brought into the bank, becoming " Bartlett, Parrott & Co." In Harrison's book there is a reproduction of one of the notes issued by the bank, " Buckingham Old Bank ". This bank seems to have become the Bucks and Oxon Union Bank, which in 1902 was taken over by Lloyds.

On 16th March, 1818 a Savings Bank was opened in the town, which is today in West Street.

The Early 19th Century

Throughout England great changes were taking place. The industrial revolution was changing life throughout the towns. New and cheaper methods of transport were needed, and in 1761 the first canal was opened. By 1830 all our present canals, with the exception of the Manchester Ship Canal had been built.

Buckingham was not left out of this fever of canal building, though it is difficult to see how our branch could have paid its way, as Buckingham was not an industrial area, and the branch ended here. Two benefactors of the church, the Marquis of Buckingham and Mr. Box, were concerned with the building of the canal, the opening being described in " The Gentleman's Magazine " 1801[9]—

" The branch of Canal from Buckingham to the Grand Junction Canal opened this day with great rejoicings. A barge with the Marquis of Buckingham, Mr. Praed and Mr. Selby (Gentlemen of the Committee), and Mr. Box, the Treasurer, accompanied by a large party of ladies and gentlemen, and a band of music, led the

[7] Harrison page 31.
[8] Harrison page 96. Lipscomb II, page 571.
[9] Harrison page 39.

way to the procession of 12 barges, laden with coal, slate, and a variety of merchandise. Upon their entrance into the basin at Buckingham they were saluted by a firing of several pieces of cannon. A numerous party were handsomely entertained by the Marquis of Buckingham at the ' Cobham Arms ' Inn on this occasion, and a liberal supply of beer was given to the populace ". This branch canal to Buckingham was nine and a quarter miles long, and was completed in eight months.

The following year, 1802, the Barracks were built, at the expense of the Marquis of Buckingham. This is a big stone building at the foot of Stowe Avenue, built originally as depot and storehouse for the Royal Bucks Militia, and later used by the Royal Bucks Yeomanry, partly as a residence.

The Manor House[10] along with much of the rest of Buckingham belonged to the owners of Stowe. Some manorial courts were held in the Manor House, and this house was also at one time used as the " Judge's Lodgings " for the assize judge, with a " Robing Room " partitioned off the hall for his use. About 1810 the Manor House became two houses, one part being a farmhouse, and the other a girls' school with two schoolrooms added at the back, which have since been demolished.

In 1805 the London Road Bridge or Long Bridge was erected by the Marquis of Buckingham, and a road connecting it to Bridge Street was cut through the " Jolly Yeoman " property. The Sheriff's Bridge, or Woolpack Bridge would be left in disuse as it was in a poor condition.

Harrison gives a description of Buckingham written in 1808. It says that " it contains 531 houses and 2,605 inhabitants, being 1,180 males and 1,425 females, of which 313 only were returned as being employed in trade or manufacture. This included the hamlets of Bourton, Gawcott and Lenborough ". At the time of the fire in 1725 there were 387 houses in Buckingham, and as 138 were destroyed in the fire, the number of houses had doubled since then. The new church is described as " elegant " and " the inside of the church is fitted up in elegant style ". The houses are not praised, however, as they were " meanly built, and many of them thatched ".

The writer of this description says that there was little trade or manufacture here, except for lace-making; but he added that there were several corn and paper mills erected on the river near the town. He did not mention that then there was a tan-yard[11], an industry which must have been of importance to the town for many years. This tan-yard which was on Hunter Street opposite the University, closed in 1861, then was reopened for a few years by a Mr. Sowerby, till it closed when he died. Another local industry of the time was the wool-yard in Hunter Street, now called

[10] Guide to Buckingham, page 29.
[11] Harrison, page 72.   V.C.H. Bucks III, page 473.

Yeomanry Hall. This was a relic of a once thriving industry. Both these yards depended on local raw materials, which was the reason why they had employed people in the town for so many years.

About this time a marble quarry was being worked at the site of the old factory, at the corner of Chandos Road and Station Road. At that time Chandos Road had not been built, and Station Road would have another name. Harrison says that several of the tombs in the old churchyard were made from local marble, as were two fireplaces that are still in the vicarage. This stone was not true marble, and was very hard and expensive to work. When the duty was taken off foreign marbles, the Buckingham stone was not a paying propostition and the industry died out.

Buckingham must have been a busy town at this time, as in 1841 a building known as the Butchers' Shambles was erected on Market Hill " to enable out-town butchers attending weekly to sell in shelter and comfort instead of being exposed to all weathers as formerly".[12] This building stood on the site of Barclays Bank, then called Butchers' Row, and according to Harrison was built at the expense of the Marquis of Buckingham, who helped the town in many other ways. The Council took over the building and rented the stalls. This was so successful that in 1833, £30 was collected, and for about the next forty years similar sums were taken in rent. As the original butchers died out, new men did not take their places, as the younger village butchers did not want to drive to weekly market. Also, possibly more butchers would have their own shops in town. In 1886 the Shambles was sold to the owners of houses in the Market Square which backed onto the Shambles, and since then part has been pulled down, but the remaining part is now the Gingerbread House. For some years the other part was a baker's shop, and it is of interest that when the present bank was being built, it was found that large, old bake ovens extended from the cellars for some distance under the Bull Ring, showing that at some earlier date, bread had been baked under the place where bulls were baited and men burnt.

The lace making, is mentioned as one of the industries of the town, and there is a tradition that it had been introduced to Buckingham-shire by Catherine of Aragon, though it had been known in England for many years before her time. Around 1570 Flemish lace makers are said to have come to England to escape oppression, and brought new ideas with them. The making of pillow lace has been a cottage industry in Buckingham for many years, but the Victoria History[13] says that at the beginning of the 19th century the women doing the work could only earn about 2/6d. a week, and the industry was decaying. Later it was revived and once again flourished, so that in 1909 Harrison could write, " At the present time there is,

[12] Harrison page 32.
[13] V.C.H. Bucks III, page 473.

however, a fair revival of custom, under the auspices of the ' Buckingham Lace Industry ' and other agencies ". Unfortunately it is now very difficult to find anyone who knows how to make Buckingham pillow lace.

1819 saw the National School built in School Lane. The School was originally intended to be built near the Barracks in West Street, but School Lane was finally chosen. Part of the building now houses the local employment office. In 1856 it was improved at a cost of £400, and in 1872 funds were raised to add an upper storey, so that the Girls' School could be upstairs while the boys were on the ground floor. A playground was added just before Harrison's book was written, when the average attendance was 90 boys and 100 girls—" the entirety of the Borough children". The infants were taught at a school on the opposite side of the road, built in 1863, with 85 children attending. This is now a builder's store.

The children attending the National School when it opened, may have seen the pillory which had stood in the Cow Fair, between the Gaol and the Red Buildings. The use of the pillory was generally abolished in England in 1816, except for perjury and subornation, and finally abolished in 1837. It is said that the Buckingham pillory was in use as late as 1794. Among Mr. Harrison's papers is this account of one who was pilloried here.
" 19th June, 1858.

John Jones of Water Stratford Woodhouse tells me he remembers when he was a boy, seeing a man (a schoolmaster from the neighbourhood, tried at the assizes here at the Old Market Hall—for some charge respecting a young lady at his school)—put in the Pillory just opposite the Horse and Groom—where the pillory was fixed—he was in for two hours—and about half an hour before he was taken out he was pelted with rotten eggs—and when they were done the people pelted him with mud, which was stop'd because there might be stones in it. Old Joe Buckingham was then Bellman of the Town and he turned the Pillory round a little bit every five or ten minutes with a spear he held in his hand—the Eggs were laid at the foot of the Pillory before he was put in—in readiness—he was not able to get out himself from exhaustion, so that Joe Buckingham and another man had to take him out and carry him back to the gaol. The Pillory was taken down when the Posts and Rails were erected for the Cowfair "

The rails and posts have since been taken away to make way for the lime trees planted by the late Mr. Egerton Hubbard in 1872.

The Buckingham to Towcester Turnpike Road was under discussion in 1824, and Mr. James Harrison, one of the Trustees of the road, received a letter from King V. Elliott, clerk, telling him of a meeting of the trustees, which was to be held on 10th January, 1825. Mr. Harrison kept the letter, which describes where the toll-houses were to be placed, the materials to be used in their construction, the thickness of walls, and the bow windows to give a view of the road. The turnpike and ' cheque ' gates are described; their position, size and shape.

In 1826 a coach called " The Union " ran from London to Buckingham, through Aylesbury and Winslow. Overnight passengers could stay at the Cobham Arms Inn or the White Hart.

In 1828 the Buckingham Horticultural Society was formed, and shows were held continuously from 1830 until the 1939-45 war, when they became a Red Cross Show.

In 1834[14] the Wesleyan chapel which had been built in Well Street, was enlarged to accommodate 350 people. In the same year the town gas works[15] were built at the entrance to London Road, at first with one gasometer. A second and larger one was added in 1859, when there was difficulty in getting the water out of the foundations. The two gasometers together could hold 30,000 cubic feet of gas, but when the works were bought by the " Bucks and Oxon District Gas Company " in 1907, the original gasometer was replaced by a telescoping one, to give an even greater capacity. These have now been demolished and removed.

Early in the 19th Century, Castle House had been owned by Philip Box, who had been concerned in the building of the canal, and had given money as a salary for a church organist. In 1835 the house was bought by Thomas Hearn, who radically altered its shape. The house at that time was quadrangular, but the north part had become dilapidated. On the advice of Sir George Gilbert Scott, the eminent architect who had been born at the Parsonage at Gawcott, the north side was pulled down, and the house left open to the gardens which rise in lawns and terraces on that side.

Gawcott

As well as Sir George Gilbert Scott, Gawcott had produced at this time another man who is well remembered. This is Mr. John West [16], who rose from humble beginnings, to be a wealthy dealer in thread lace. Gawcott at that time had 500 inhabitants but no church. Mr. West gave between £4,000 and £5,000 to build and endow a chapel, which was consecrated on the 14th May, 1807, with the Rev. Thomas Scott as Minister. The chapel was to cost more than was hoped, however, as, according to Lipscomb, " The foundation having been injudiciously laid, and the workmanship ill conducted, it was found necessary to rebuild the whole fabric ".

There would be some recriminations in Gawcott over this, but the money was raised, the church rebuilt and also a house built for the incumbent. Twelve acres of glebe land were bought with

[14] Harrison, page 55.
[15] Harrison page 81.
[16] Lipscomb II, page 591.   Sheahan page 250.

£1,100 granted by the Governors of Queen Anne's Bounty, and £228 raised by public subscription in 1817.

John West died in 1814, leaving money to be invested to give an income of £30 to be used for the poor of Gawcott.

The Inclosure Act of 1821 included Prebend End, Gawcott and Maids Moreton. In Gawcott, allotments were assigned to the Impropriators and the vicar in lieu of tithes. The poor of Gawcott lost their ancient rights to cut furze on the waste land, and instead received an allotment of 14 acres.

Stowe

Richard Grenville, Earl Temple, died in 1779 after a carriage accident in the grounds of Stowe. He was succeeded by his nephew George, son of George Grenville, politician and Prime Minister.

George, the new owner of Stowe, soon obtained a license to take the name of Nugent and Temple as well as his own name. He had married Mary Nugent in 1775. In 1782 he became Lord Lieutenant of the county, and in 1784 was made Marquis of Buckingham, and in 1786 a Knight of the Garter. He had two periods as Lord Lieutenant of Ireland; during the second one, which started in 1787, he came into conflict with the Irish Parliament when he refused to transmit an address from that body, to the Prince of Wales, asking him to act as Regent during his father's illness. He was censured in both Houses of the Irish Parliament, but the king's recovery strengthened his position and he dismissed many members who had opposed him, and even used corruption to support his position. He resigned in 1789, returned to England and retired from political life.

He had become Earl Nugent on the death of his father-in-law in 1788, and after his retirement, lived at Stowe collecting art and manuscripts. He was visited there in 1808 by Louis XVIII of France and his family, who were living as exiles at Hartwell House near Aylesbury.

He was succeeded in 1813 by his son Richard, who in 1816 held the office of Deputy-President of the Board of Trade, and was later Paymaster-General and Lord Lieutenant of Buckinghamshire.

He married Lady Anne Brydges, daughter and heiress of the last Duke of Chandos. Through her he received the title of Baron Kinloss, and on her father's death he was made Duke of Buckingham and Chandos. He spent money profusely on improvements at Stowe and in 1834 was obliged to sell some furniture and works of art.

A Reformed Corporation

The Reform Bill passed by the Whig government in 1832 caused a major redistribution of seats in parliament. Some old constituencies, e.g. Wendover, lost their seats, while seats were given to places which were previously inadequately represented, e.g. Manchester, Birmingham and Leeds. This Bill affected Buckingham less than might have been expected, as it was left with two members of parliament, but the boundary of the electoral district was altered to include Maids Moreton, Thornborough, Padbury, Hillesden, Preston Bissett-cum-Cowley, Tingewick and Radclive-cum-Chackmore[17].

Before this Bill, the bailiff and principal burgesses had the sole rights of electing the members of parliament for the borough, but at this time, the franchise was altered throughout England, so that in the boroughs the qualification was that of the £10 occupier, which in general served to enfranchise the middle and lower-middle classes, but not the artisans. In 1862 Sheahan wrote that there were 360 voters in the Parliamentary Borough of Buckingham, a very different picture from 1831.

The Reform Bill altered the way in which the people of England were represented in parliament, but change was needed in local government. A Royal Commission was appointed to report on the conditions of local government of the boroughs. The commission reported on 285 towns of which 246 were held to be boroughs[18]. One of these was Buckingham. Lipscomb quotes at length the part concerning Buckingham, which was at that time acting under the conditions of the Queen Mary Charter, except where these had been changed by the Reform Bill of 1832. The bailiff and burgesses are mentioned in the report, and how they were elected. The bailiff received no salary, but was allowed to " receive to his own use some small quit rents, the tolls of the market, and the piccage and stallage, amounting in the whole to £63 a year ".

Although the bailiff was elected by the townsfolk from two burgesses named by the corporation, in latter years other considerations had crept in. " During the time of the late Marquess of Buckingham, it was the practice of the Corporation, upon such occasions, to send three names to the Marquess, of which he selected one; or if all were agreeable to him, he left it to the Corporation to select; and he has ever since been usually nominated by the Duke's steward. No one has ever been elected without the Duke's sanction, and under an actual or implied engagement to resign in case of not using his elective franchise as the Duke may require ". In other words, the Duke controlled the chief officer of the town.

A bye-law had been passed in 1822, fixing the fees and expenses paid on the election of Bailiffs and Burgesses.

[17] Sheahan page 228.
[18] The Constitutional History of Modern Britain by D. L. Keir, page 422.

" ON BAILIFF'S ELECTION "

							£	s.	d.
Under Bailiff	...	...	...	...	...	...	1	1	0
Town Clerk	...	...	...	...	...	...	1	1	0
Deputy Steward	...	...	...	...	...	...		10	6
Chairman ...	...	...	...	...	...	...		10	6
Poll Clerk ...	...	...	...	...	...	...		10	6
Gaoler ...	...	...	...	...	...	...		5	0
Hall Keeper ...	...	...	...	...	...	...		5	0
Crier ...	...	...	...	...	...	...		2	6
Watchman ...	...	...	...	...	...	...		2	6
Ringers ...	...	...	...	...	...	...	2	2	0
Music... ...	...	...	...	...	...	...	2	11	6
May Bushes ...	...	...	...	...	...	...		10	6
Election Breakfasts for the Constables, etc.					...	...	5	3	0
Same at Christmas	...	...	...	...	...	...	5	3	0
Same on quitting office	...	...	...	...	...	...	5	3	0
Beer at twenty-six houses ...	...	...	...	...	...	7	16	0
Constables' Dinners	...	...	...	...	...	...	11	11	0
Sundry Treating ...	...	...	...	...	...	5	0	0
							£49	8	6

Besides this the bailiff was expected to give a venison-feast during his year of office ".

The expenses on the election of a burgess were less than those for the bailiff.

" ON THE ELECTION OF A BURGESS "

							£	s.	d.
The Town Clerk	...	...	...	...	...	...	5	5	0
Ringers ...	...	...	...	...	...	...	1	11	6
Under Bailiff	...	...	...	...	...	...	1	1	0
Gaoler ...	...	...	...	...	...	...		10	6
Crier ...	...	...	...	...	...	...		2	6
Watchman ...	...	...	...	...	...	...		2	6
Each Blue-coat Man and Green-gown Man (sixteen altogether) ½ peck loaf, and 1½ lb. of meat, about							2	0	0
Two barrels of Ale for public distribution			...	...	9	0	0
							£19	13	0

The constables seem to have done quite well out of the election of a bailiff, but are not even mentioned in the election expenses of a burgess. The report points out that before the Reform Act of 1832, the bailiff and burgesses were the electorate of the borough, and that for the previous thirty years " the greatest number of electors polled . . . . was eleven. In modern times, this franchise has always been exercised under the control and management of the Duke of Buckingham and his ancestors; and lists have been published, shewing that (e.g. in 1830) every member of the Corporation was, either directly or indirectly, connected with, and dependent upon, the Duke of Buckingham ".

The commissioners summed up their opinion of the function of the Corporation, " The Corporation of Buckingham has, for a long time, served as an instrument for enabling the patron of the borough to return two members to Parliament, and for nothing more. As a Corporation, it has never discharged any of the functions of town government, for it has scarcely any revenue ". The report then describes the inadequacies in the various courts held in the town.

At this time there were eight constables for the borough, " selected by the bailiff out of the householders. These constables have no remuneration. Two night-watchmen are supported by private subscription among the inhabitants ". Harrison gives the text of a document dated 1792, of an agreement to appoint a Watch within the borough, the expenses to be defrayed by voluntary contributions. The contributors include Philip Box who gave 3/-, John Bartlett, who also gave 3/-, R. Adcock who gave 6d., and many others, who together gave £5 3s. 11d. quarterly.

The borough gaol is reported in 1835, " though a capacious building, is little used, is under the superintendence of the bailiff. The Corporation appoint a gaoler ". It was to the credit of the town that the gaol was little used.

The Corporation are said to have no property or revenue whatsoever, except tolls, which are let at £33 a year, some quit-rents for £5 a year, and £30 from the Duke of Buckingham, which came under the name of " Rent of the Shambles in the Market-House ". Of this income £5 went to Christ's Hospital, which left £63 as the income for the Corporation, and all this went to the bailiff for his own use. The report states that " It will be seen by the table which is given above, of the expenses of his election in office, that nearly the whole of it is spent in fees to inferior officers of the Corporation, and in idle and unnecessary feasting. Without the ' Rent of the Shambles ' from the patron of the borough, it is obvious that the whole income of the Corporation would not be nearly sufficient to cover the bailiff's annual expenses; and this circumstance may perhaps furnish an explanation of the apparently singular fact, that the Duke of Buckingham should hold the butchers' shambles, as tenants to the Corporation, at a rent of £30 a year. It could not be discovered, that any profit was made of the shambles by the lessee, or indeed that any tolls were received by him, or on his account ". (This is a different account of the ownership and renting of the Shambles, from that given by Harrison).

These were hard words about the Duke of Buckingham and his obedient Corporation, but it should be said that the report of the

Royal Commissioners condemned the existing systems of local government so strongly, that they can be suspected of prejudging the issue[18]. The report also tells us that " the Corporation appoint the master to the Free Grammar School, with a salary of £11 a-year, and a house rent-free. They also appoint six green-coat and ten blue-coat men, the objects of certain eleemosynary endowments."

As a result of this report, 178 of the investigated towns were brought within the Municipal Corporations Act of 1835, which applied to towns which were not yet incorporated. Borough government was in the control of councils elected by ratepayers. Buckingham had the office of bailiff abolished and replaced by a mayor. The council consisted of four alderman who held office for six years, and twelve councillors holding office for three years. The office of steward of the borough was retained, and in 1835 was held by the Duke of Buckingham. The under-bailiff had his duties combined with those of mace-bearer. The town-clerk, who had not been mentioned in the Mary Charter or the Charles Charter, was appointed by the steward in 1835, and acted as his deputy.

Buckingham was brought into line with the rest of the country. The corruption, venison feasts and constables' breakfasts had to stop.

CHAPTER XI

VICTORIAN BUCKINGHAM 1835—1908

AFTER the Municipal Corporation Act came into effect, the town was no longer under the political domination of Stowe. Much of the town was still owned by them, but the electorate could vote freely.

The population was rising rapidly, from 2,605 in 1801 to 3,610 in 1831, and a maximum of 4,054 in 1841. Local industries were started, some of which were successful for a short time, and there was a great deal of building to keep pace with the increase of population.

In 1835 a ' Union ' Workhouse was built on Stratford Road[1], a stone building which has been demolished. It was designed by Sir G. G. Scott, cost £8,215 and could accommodate 135 paupers. An Isolation Fever Ward was added about 30 years later, and a Board Room and a ' Casual Ward ' in 1898, ' near the entrance gates, with separate cells for each caller, in which they must perform an allotted task in return for board and lodging, bath, etc.'

A semi-circular Superintendent's residence, also designed by Sir G. G. Scott, was added to the old gaol in 1839. This faces the market square and has had many uses. In 1892 when the Borough Police amalgamated with the County Police, the gaol was condemned and a new police station and lock-up, which is still used, was built on Moreton Road. There was a suggestion at this time that the old gaol should be pulled down, but it was converted into a Fire Engine Station, then was used as an ammunition store by the local Rifle Corps, and part is now used as an electrical sub-station.

The Collapse at Stowe

Things were not going so well at Stowe. The first Duke of Buckingham and Chandos, despite his marriage to an heiress, had been obliged to sell some furniture and works of art in 1834. His son, the second Duke, was as extravagant as his ancestors, without the means to support his tastes. He had invested much of his money in land, which decreased in value after the repeal of the Corn Laws in 1846. Before this, in 1840 Queen Adelaide had visited Stowe, after passing through Buckingham on the way, where 800 school-children sang the National Anthem, and all admired a triple arch in the market place which carried the loyal sentence, " God Help Queen Adelaide " ! In 1844 there had been huge and expensive celebrations at the coming of age of the Duke's son.

The following year Queen Victoria came to Stowe for several

---

[1] Harrison page 38.

days. Buckingham was decorated for the occasion, and Stowe put on a good show, but by this time the fortunes of the family had changed, the bailiffs were in the house, but loyally agreed to wear the uniform of the Duke's retainers while the Queen was there. In 1848 there was a great sale of the contents of the house, and most of the estates. The sale lasted 40 days and realised £75,562 4s. 6d. After the sale the Duke lived in retirement, but between 1850 and 1860 he offended the Queen by publishing extracts from some of his manuscripts as memoirs of the Court of George III, the Regency and George IV.

The third and last Duke of Buckingham and Chandos was a politician like his ancestors, and was, at different times, Governor of Madras, Chairman of the London North-Western Railway, and Chairman of the Executive Committee of the Great Exhibition. He had simple tastes, lived economically and managed to settle his debts and even recover some of the family treasures. When he died in 1889 many of his titles died with him, but the estates of Stowe and the Scottish Barony of Kinloss went to his daughter, Mary.

Developments in Buckingham

The Lord's Bridge, the wooden bridge that had spanned the river in Prebend End on the road to Gawcott, was often under water when the river rose. The present brick, double-arched bridge was erected in 1846, and in 1851 the old Castle Bridge in Tingewick Road was replaced by the present Tingewick Road Bridge. The London Road Bridge or Long Bridge was built in 1805 when the old Sheriff's Bridge or Woolpack Bridge fell into disrepair. A new main road was cut to join the Long Bridge to the London Road, and a smaller, wooden foot-bridge was built near the Woolpack, where a ford was also made. This wooden bridge became rotten in time and was replaced in 1864 by the present iron foot-bridge.

The Duke of Buckingham and Chandos had for many years resisted the idea of a railway passing through his property—it would spoil the seclusion of Stowe. Buckingham was therefore not included in the main network of railways that was developed early in the century. The position of the town as a stopping place for coaches between London and the north, was not repeated in the plan of the railways. A branch line connected the town to the main railway system in 1850, but the industrial developments which would have come from a position on a main line were lost. Buckingham continued as a pleasant, quiet, market town.

The booking office for the station was at first on the far side of the line, but when in 1853 the Duke of Buckingham built Chandos Road to connect the town with the railway, the station was moved to the near side of the track. Station Road was built to connect Gawcott Road with the railway in 1861, and taken over by the Corporation about the end of the century.

The Old Latin School fell into a state of disrepair during the first half of the century, so that in 1855, £95 was needed to repair the master's house and appoint a new master. The trustees were not sure of public support in re-establishing the school, so waited until 1857 before making a public appeal for money to repair and plaster the walls, open Archdeacon Ruding's window, put a new stone head to the doorway, remove the flat ceiling and erect a bell turret.

The schoolroom was again restored in 1879, and the school continued under schoolmasters Mr. Cockram, Mr. McCulloch and Mr. Cox until in 1907 it was transferred to the new buildings on the Chandos Road, buildings which now house the County Junior School.

The Board School in Well Street was built in 1879, and is now Buckingham First School.

Churches and Chapels

The 19th century saw a number of churches and chapels being built in Buckingham. In 1842 a Baptist Chapel was built in Podd's Lane, now Moreton Road. This chapel was later used by the Salvation Army, and Miss Alice Palmer remembers that the first Salvation Army people to come to Buckingham were arrested for disturbing the peace by playing their band in the market place. They were sent to gaol at Aylesbury, but on their return, they were welcomed by many of the townsfolk.

A Primitive Methodist Chapel was built in 1844 in Prebend End. This was a brick building, and cost £200. In 1862 Sheahan wrote that ' The Society of Friends have a disused Meeting-House in the Cow Fair'. This is remembered by the name, 'Quakers Orchard '.

A new Congregational Church was built in 1857 at a cost of £2,000. It was built on the site of a former chapel which had been built in 1700. A Sunday School and Classrooms were added between 1876 and 1879, making a well-built block.

The parish church was observed to be developing cracks in the walls, and when the Rev. W. F. Norris came to the town in 1862 he ' found this church in a dilapidated condition and utterly unfit for its purpose '.[2] The foundations of the church did not reach the bedrock, they rested on a thin layer of rock which had clay underneath, Sir G. G. Scott, the local architect, was called in and designed supporting buttresses which went down to the bedrock 14 feet deep.

The alterations to the nave, changing it from classical lines to modern Gothic, took place about the same time. Columns were added of local marble, and the entire appearance was altered. The money for the chancel was given by the Duke of Buckingham and Chandos, and he also helped to pay for the repairs to the church.

[2] Notes from the Rev. J. H. B. Elkerton.

A side-aisle was given by the late Lord Addington, and stained glass windows were given at different times. The three decker pulpit was removed.

A chapel was built on Bone Hill in 1865. This was originally used as a Day School and Mission Chapel, but is now demolished. The Wesleyan Chapel in Well Street was found to be defective structurally several years ago and a new building was erected on the site.

A Roman Catholic College was built on the London Road in 1894, and was originally intended for boys who proposed to join the Franciscan Order. A church was built in the grounds in 1912, and was the Catholic parish church for the district. The school for years used as a boarding and day school is now closed.

The old churchyard was closed as a burial ground in 1853, and a new cemetery opened on the Brackley Road in 1856, and was extended in 1898. We are not told of the arrangements for those who died between 1853 and 1856, except that unfilled family vaults could still be used in the old churchyard.

A big step in modern progress was taken in 1854 when a local newspaper, the " Buckingham Advertiser " was started. A little later, during an invasion scare by Napoleon III in 1859, a Volunteer Rifle Corps was established. However, ordinary life went on and a bathing place in the river was organised the next year; ' a portion of the stream at the bottom of Mr. Tibbett's yard (where it enters the town from Brackley) was cleaned out '. This was behind the Corner House in West Street. This bathing place was used for about 10 years. About 1891 another bathing place was arranged near the Goods Station.

The marble quarry which had been worked early in the century did not last long, and a ' Hunting Establishment ' under the denomination of the " Buckingham Hotel Company " was built on the site. This was abandoned and in 1857 became the Castle Iron Works or Foundry, which is described by Sheahan[3]. This business was managed by Mr. Thomas Rickett, who was an engineer. Harrison says that the original idea was to make harrows, ploughs, etc., but that the manager, who was a theorist, invented and manufactured instead steam road carriages. Mr. Rickett must have been a practical man as well as a theorist, as his steam carriages worked well. Sheahan says, ' After a few months a locomotive steam engine was made, of eight horse power, for Mr. Beards of Stowe, which travelled over the land as well as the roads, and was used for ploughing, thrashing, etc. . . . . . Another steam carriage was ordered for Belgium, and the Prince of Wales having expressed a wish to see it, Mr. Rickett drove it by the high road to Windsor, and on the 9th January, 1860, it was there inspected by the Queen and her royal household . . . . It has ample room for three persons in front, and for a stoker behind, and runs at an average speed of ten miles an hour. On good roads it gets over sixteen miles an hour '. The

[3] Sheahan pages 231-232.

Earl of Caithness bought a similar carriage from Buckingham and travelled 150 miles in two days ' over some of the steepest roads in Scotland '.

After the making of steam engines, the premises were used as a Steam Corn and Cake Mill, and then the Bucks Direct Dairy Supply Co. took over and for some years sent farm produce to wholesale London establishments ' but eventually (as the Londoners claimed too great a share of the profits) this idea was abandoned '.[4]

The next people to buy the buildings were the Condensed Peptonised Milk Co. Ltd., who started work in 1892. They used local milk, processing it into a number of products. The premises were later occupied by the Wilts United Dairies for many years, until they ceased to use the building which was later bought by Cementone.

The tanyard had ceased in 1861, and the wool yard some time later. A shoe factory was run for some time in what is now Markham's warehouse, and a corn chandler's business at Chapman's photographers '. At the north end of the town were mills for superphosphate and bones, and there were limestone quarries in the vicinity. In the town were maltings, and a brewery in School Lane.

Houses were built on the new Chandos Road, including one 'in the Italian style with a lofty campanile tower', later demolished to make way for Chandos Close Estate. The town was busy, and a Literary and Scientific Society met regularly in the town hall. This society possessed a small museum and a library of 700 to 800 volumes. The Rev. Roundell lectured to the Society on the history of the town.

A second newspaper, the " Buckingham Express " was started in 1865, and in the following year the Red Buildings, erected after the 1725 fire, were pulled down. A Nursing Home was started in Castle Street in 1868, and in 1887 was moved to the present hospital building, designed by Sir G. G. Scott.

Castle House was altered in 1881, when the ' Great Parlour ' was restored, an oak beam being added, and a partition removed so that the north window was included in the room.

The Electric Light Works came to Buckingham in 1888, first at the Town Mills, moving to the Tanyard in 1897, and to School Lane in 1904, when they made a contract to light the streets. They moved to Well Street in 1928. Harrison tells us that until 1893 the drinking water for the town had come from five public and some private wells, but some of these became contaminated through the introduction of cesspools, and the Corporation decided to provide water works and sewerage. The water came from Akeley to a storage tank at Maids Moreton; bore holes later gave more water to the scheme. The Drainage Works were carried out in 1896, some of the mains in the town being nearly 20 feet deep causing

[4] Harrison page 70.

trouble, but it was completed in the end.

Local bank notes ceased to be issued in 1902 when the ' Bucks and Oxon Bank ' was taken over by Lloyds. In 1906 School Boards were abolished and Board Schools became Council Schools.

A Smaller Population

In 1841 the population of Buckingham was 4,054, a great increase over the figure of 2,605 which had been recorded in 1801. The town did not continue to grow, as the population figures show:—

1841	...	4,054	1881	...	3,585
1851	...	4,020	1891	...	3,364
1861	...	3,849	1901	...	3,152
1871	...	3,703	1911	...	3,282

The geographical position of the town in the northern part of the county would affect its chances of remaining the county town. Aylesbury with its more central position had natural advantages. Buckingham did not give up the fight easily. When James Harrison was mayor a ' Memorial to her Majesty's Justices of the Peace for the County of Buckingham '[5] was sent, asking that the Summer Assizes should still be held at Buckingham, as the town depended largely on the custom that came with the assizes to the local innkeepers and tradesmen.

The fact that the main railway line did not pass through Buckingham would hinder the town's progress, as industries would be established in towns with quicker rail connections with London.

Though a number of small industries were tried in the town, few succeeded for any length of time, and there must have been intermittent unemployment for much of the 19th century. The financial collapse of Stowe would affect the town adversely, as for many years much of the trade had been connected with the Stowe family.

The representation of Buckingham in parliament had been altered by the Representation of the People's Act of 1867, in which Buckingham was reduced from two members to one. In the 1885 Redistribution of the Seats Act, Buckingham was merged with the north of the county.

A few years after this Act the Duke of Buckingham and Chandos died, and the estate of Stowe was left in the hands of his daughter, Mary, Lady Kinloss. In 1890 she let Stowe to the Comte de Paris, heir to the throne of France, who lived there for four years. During his stay, notices at the railway station in Buckingham were in French and English for the convenience of his many visitors.

The funeral of the Comte de Paris in 1894 was very splendid. The huge black hearse was drawn by magnificent black horses bedecked with black plumes. There were many coaches of mourners. Buckingham had seldom seen such a sight.

Lady Kinloss came back to live in part of Stowe in 1901, as the twentieth century was beginning.

[5] Harrison's Notes.

CHAPTER XII

PRESENT DAY BUCKINGHAM

THE population of Buckingham had been 4,054 in 1841 and had fallen to 3,282 in 1911. The industrial progress that had helped so many towns in the country had not greatly affected Buckingham. Little progress had been made commercially, and it remained predominantly an agricultural market town. The limited travel facilities which existed before the first World War made Buckingham a focal point for the local farmers, and early in the century reasonable markets were enjoyed.

In those days there was still a calf market on Mondays in Well Street with the pens against the raised footpath. There were tugs-of-war across the river at the back of the White Hart, and in the winter there were snow battles between the children of the Well Street School and the National School. The fair which came to the Market Square had confetti and squibs that were thrown at the people on the roundabouts. The caravans were drawn by horses and the children's roundabouts were turned by ponies.

Housing development came to a standstill with the Great War, and many local people had soldiers billeted in their properties. The soldiers drilled in the Market Square and children with sticks instead of guns came to march with them.

With the return of the troops from the fighting the Council gave top priority to housing, and the Bourtonville estate was erected, with 68 houses on the road connecting London Road to Bourton Road. The population figures continued to fall, from 3,282 in 1911 to 3,060 in 1921, and 3,083 in 1931, when an economic depression was affecting the western world. This depression caused a lull in building in the town, but from 1934 onwards many local people had private houses built in London, Bourton and Stratford Roads and also on Stowe Avenue.

Sporting activities were not lacking locally and for a short time greyhound racing took place in Tingewick Road and Westfields. There were also film shows in the Town Hall until 1934 when the Chandos cinema was built.

In the inter-war years Buckingham saw many changes. The Council built houses on Westfields and on Addington Road, connecting Stratford and Moreton Roads.

In 1935 the County Secondary School opened and in 1938 the National Schools in School Lane, which had opened in 1819 and 1863, closed. The present post office was built in 1939, but before this, many buildings had been used as the post office including the former Cobham Arms in West Street, on which the words POST OFFICE can still be seen near the top of the building.

Speculative building was not successful at this time and a number of Gawcott Fields properties had to be let. Just as war was declared several private houses and bungalows were being built at Mount Pleasant on Lenborough Road.

With the Second World War came evacuees from London and other cities, buying unsold properties as homes and business premises, and there was a minor industrial boom. Many members of the armed forces were stationed in the district and the Chandos Road cinema played to packed houses. The Oddfellows Hall and the Methodist Guild Rooms were used as canteens for the forces. Buckingham was busy.

Post-War Buckingham

After the war, in 1945, some factories moved back to London but some remained, such as Leslie Hartridge Ltd. in Tingewick Road and Messrs. E. and F. Richardson Ltd. at Castle Mills, now much extended into Sigma Coatings.

The Borough Council started a large housing development on the Overn Hill Estate with a new road from West Street to Moreton Road. More roads and houses have since been added including some pensioners' bungalows in Cobham Close. In recent years two groups of flats for retired people have been built, Chandos Court overlooking the park and North End Court.

With peaceful conditions new private houses were built in various areas in the outskirts of the town. These houses were sold more easily than other houses before the war.

As new people came to live in the town, the population rose from 3942 in 1951 to 4379 in 1961 then 4750 in 1964. These extra people were buying the new houses and many were working in the new industries that had come to the town. These included milk bottling, the making of carpets, electronic equipment and plastic toys.

In 1959 Wipac moved from Bletchley to a large, well-designed factory in Buckingham, with gardens next to the road. The 500 employees now make magnetoes for lawn mowers and outboard engines, ignition and other equipment for the motor industry, electronic components for telephone exchanges and gas ignitors.

Soon after the beginning of the second world war Leslie Hartridge moved his business from London to an old water mill and other buildings in the grounds of Richardson's paint factory, but by 1941 there was another move to the present factory on Tingewick Road. After the war business was expanded by producing a wider range of diesel and vehicle testing equipment.

Hartridges, part of the Lucas Group since 1956, now occupies a 6 acre site, and the original 10 people from London has grown to over 350. The turnover exceeds £10,000,000 a year, 70% of the main products being exported. This achievement has won Queens Awards to Industry in 1969 and 1974 and a Design Council Award in 1983.

E. and F. Richardson Ltd. moved to Buckingham in 1939. The company has a modern factory in Tingewick Road where the paint is produced.

By 1974 the company was taken over by Sigma Coatings as many of Richardson's products were already to Sigma's formulations, and a merger made economic sense.

The award of the important Thames Barrier Contract to the company was a result of the joining of the two companies, both highly regarded technically. In 1983 the firm of Allweather Paints was acquired.

Cementone Ltd. was moved to Buckingham in 1968, and its origins go back to 1776 when the company, Joseph Freeman and Sons Ltd. was formed. It was one of the earliest companies to deal in paints and printing inks, then in the 1870s dealt in building chemicals and pigments. In 1976 a company called Wykamol, dealing with the treatment and preservation of old and new buildings, was absorbed into the Buckingham operation.

Cementone combined with Beaver in 1981 and the resulting big company, called Cementone-Beaver with centres at Buckingham and Leeds, produces the largest range in the United Kingdom of cement additives and colourants, adhesives, wood preservatives and finishes, and paints for the home use.

Products from the company's factories, including the new one in Tingewick Road, are in use in many places including the Albert Hall in London, the Airport in Abu Dhabi, H.M.S. Victory and the Royal Temples of Katmandu.

The cattle market in the High Street was discontinued towards the end of 1969 as trade was reduced, and now part of the old cattle market is used as a bus station with a bus shelter.

During these years there had been even greater changes at Stowe than in Buckingham. The final sale of the estate and the contents took place in 1921, and two years later the house was opened once again as Stowe School, a public school for boys. In 1924 Stowe Avenue was presented to the school by the action of a number of old Etonians. In 1927 the chapel foundation stone was laid by Queen Mary, who passed through Buckingham, and the chapel opened on June 11, 1929 by Prince George (later the Duke of Kent).

Before the Second World War Buckingham was visited by the Prince of Wales, who became King Edward VIII, later Duke of Windsor. There have been several post-war royal visits to the town. In 1963 Queen Elizabeth the Queen Mother went to Stowe, which was celebrating its fortieth anniversary, then to the Latin School to open their new buildings.

For some years the branch railway line from Bletchley to Buckingham carried very few passengers. The town station won awards for its flower beds, but that did not help when the Beeching cuts came and the station closed in 1964. However, it was reopened for the royal train which brought the Queen and the Duke of

Edinburgh to the town on the 4th of April 1966 to visit the Bull Ring, the Town Hall and to drive past the Old Gaol.

The charter fairs continue to be held, the roundabouts and stalls have spread along the Market Square and High Street so that for two weekends in October the Saturday market stalls are in Moreton Road.

Buckingham joined in the successful campaign to prevent the Third London Airport being sited in the Wing area, just a few miles to the south east of the town. Money was given and time spent very willingly.

The town was twinned with Joinville in France, and the annual pancake race which was held in the Market Square on Shrove Tuesday was changed to a race between Buckingham and Bells Corner in Canada.

Buckingham Town Football Club bought its own football field, the town bought the tennis courts, bowling green and land for a park beside the river, and also Maids Moreton Avenue at the north end of the town.

In 1963 the Royal Latin School moved to new buildings at Brookfields and the old buildings in Chandos Road became the Junior School, leaving Buckingham First School in Well Street.

A new Methodist Chapel replaced the old one in Well Street, and a new Catholic Church in Chandos Road was built, and the church on London Road no longer used. In Verney Close on the river side of the Market Square, a court house was built in 1961, then a library, health centre, nurses' flats and recently a Red Cross day centre.

The old fire station near the hospital was replaced by a new one on Bourton Road in 1973, with firemen's houses alongside.

Buckingham Borough Development Co. Ltd.

In 1964 there was a proposal to build a new city, Milton Keynes, and it was expected that Buckingham would grow as a result, from 4750 people to 15000 as the new city developed. The first big new housing estate, Page Hill, was started in 1970 with a first and junior school for that end of the town, and the Summerlee Estate was built beside Moreton Road.

The main difficulty in expanding the town was that the town's sewage system was already used to capacity, and a new £1,000,000 sewage system, which the town could not afford, was needed for any expansion. A plan by which the Land Commission would help, was dropped in 1970 when the Land Commission was abolished.

The County Council and the Buckingham Borough Council decided to promote a company to deal with the land owners, to assemble and service land for development, sell the more valuable, serviced land at a profit to the developers and use its share of the profits for new sewage works and other things to help the town.

On the 26th of March 1971 the Buckingham Borough Development

117

Co. Ltd. was formed and was at that time a unique scheme to solve the problems of land assembly.

The company has dealt with the land for Stratford Fields and Badgers Estates. Over 440 houses were sold in these estates by March 1982. Meadway Estate near Wipac was developed by Wipac and Edgar Taylor Ltd.

The road outside these estates was paid for by the developers and Buckingham Borough Development Co. It forms part of an essential ring road which was completed by the county, who also built a new bridge and road connecting Stratford Fields and Badgers. As well as the new sewage works, trunk sewage, part of the ring road and roads in the development areas, the company has given £100,000 to the new community hall and £30,000 for the railway footpath. It is also encouraging industry to come to Buckingham.

Local Government

In 1963, when other water supplies joined to form the Bucks Water Board, the borough retained control of its own water supply.

Local government was reorganised in 1974; Buckingham, Aylesbury and four rural district councils were abolished and afterwards only Buckingham retained a town council. At the same time the Buckingham Borough water supplies were taken over by the Anglian Water Authority.

The most recent change in local government is that since 1982 Gawcott has its own parish council but is still represented on the Buckingham Town Council.

Parliamentary constituency boundaries were altered for the last general election, separating the Buckingham area from Milton Keynes.

The University

When Mr. Fred Pooley, the first manager of Buckingham Borough Development Co., met one of the planners of a new independent university college, he suggested Buckingham as the site, and when this town was chosen, the Buckingham Borough Development Co. helped by acquiring the chosen property on Hunter Street and holding it until the university was ready to take it over as the University College at Buckingham.

Old buildings were renovated by the university, the old Barracks of the Royal Bucks Hussars became the Library building, the Commander's house because Yeomanry House, a row of cottages became Istra Cottages and other property was restored and improved, producing a very attractive area of the town beyond the old churchyard.

The Principal, Professor Max Beloff, the librarian and other staff were appointed. A 2 year course, 8 terms of 10 weeks, was planned (which was more than the 72 weeks in a 3 year degree course at Oxford or Cambridge), students being awarded a license at its successful conclusion.

After some delays, in February 1976 the first 67 students started their first academic year. They lived in the Istra Cottages and houses in estates on the outskirts of the town. The secondary school annexe, formerly a Franciscan seminary and boarding school on London Road, was bought in 1977 and converted as living quarters for staff and students, with a library and other public rooms. Since then new student accommodation has been built on either side of Hunter Street, and student and staff dining rooms and public rooms are in use in the old Town Mill which has been rebuilt and extended.

The university has many contacts with the town. As well as lectures for students, concerts and some services attended by townsfolk are held in the Radcliffe Centre, formerly the United Reformed Church, which was restored by the university. The Natural History Society and the Buckingham lectures are open to the public.

The contacts are two sided. The Friends of the University have given their support in many ways. The Rotarians and others help by entertaining overseas students.

There are now 500 students working at the university which received its charter in 1983.

Buckingham Hospital

Buckingham Hospital, above the High Street, was given to the town in 1886 by J. G. Hubbard later Lord Addington, and was privately supported until 1948 when it was taken over by the National Health Service.

In 1966 the League of Friends of Buckingham Hospital was formed to fight threats of closure which hung over this and other small hospitals. In 1977 only one consultant's clinic remained at the hospital as consultants holding other clinics had retired. Dr. C. R. Brown and other local doctors found that several new consultants at Stoke Mandeville would like to hold clinics at the hospital. The Area Health Authority though willing could not afford the staff needed for the clinics. It was agreed that if the League of Hospital Friends provided £10,000 a year for 5 years, to pay the wages of a hospital secretary, nurse and radiographer, clinics could be held in Buckingham with the Area Health Authority covering other expenses.

Following a town meeting on the 9th of May 1977, more than half the money was promised for 5 years, including a large monthly sum from Wipac, which still continues. Other local companies, the university and 250 families also provided money, and many still contribute.

By 1982 £107,264 had been raised and 10 regular consultant clinics were being held. Two thousand members of the League in

Buckingham and the surrounding villages still contribute annually, some by cheque, but most to the 66 door to door collectors. Some of the money was raised by football matches and other social events.

This money provided wages, a new car park, a lift, installation of X-ray equipment, furniture and many other things. Many people have worked hard to make the hospital the busy and happy place it now is, and many are now saved a weary day travelling to Stoke Mandeville and back.

There are now plans for more expansion of the hospital.

This has been a unique way of increasing the activities of a cottage hospital at a time when some small hospitals are closing.

Recent Days

In the 1970s the old workhouse near the hospital and the railway station were demolished. Two banks and shops have replaced old buildings in the Market Square.

Castle House had been used as a council office by the old Borough Council and the garden was open to the public, but after the local government reorganisation it was sold by Aylesbury Vale District Council. They also sold the old Town Hall, leaving the town without a public hall for some years. Recently the new community hall has been built behind the High Street, next to the new telephone building.

Selective education remains in the town, with the old grammar school and the secondary school, which now has an Adult Education Centre nearby.

In 1979 Buckingham First School celebrated its centenary by turning the old part of the school into a museum for the day, and inviting all present and past staff and pupils to come. They came, filling the school and playground for a wonderful day.

Since 1969 the carpet factory has closed, as have the Cooperative Milk Factory and Wilts United Dairies, whose premises in Chandos Road have been taken over by Adrian Hornsey, formerly an antique dealer in the town and now an exporter.

The Buckingham Borough Development Co. owns the site of the former goods station and land beside the ring road, which is planned for future industrial use, the latter being already serviced for development.

Buckingham has progressed in recent years, but it still remains at heart a quiet, country market town.

The new city of Milton Keynes, only a few miles away, could change the town in many ways. In any event, however, it will surely still bear the stamp of its long and interesting history.

INDEX

James I 50, 55, 74, 76, 78.
James II 55, 66, 74, 76, 77, 78, 79, 85.
James IV 38.
John of the Mill 23.
John, King 21, 41.
John, St. the Baptist 35, 36, 39, 79, 97.
Jefferies, Judge 70, 72, 76.
Jeffrey's Map 19.
Jeffrey's, Thomas 73, 74.
Jenkins, Mr. 88.
Joinville 117.
Jolly Yeoman 99.
Jones, John 101.
Josslyn, John 35.
Jutes 13.

Kecketan 54.
Kensington Gardens 78.
Kent, Nathaniel 77.
Kerdyf, Richard de 28.
Kerry 65.
Kew, John 69.
Kings Head 53, 89.
Kings Sutton 14, 28, 36.
Kinross, Baron 103, 109.
Kirby Moorside 77.
Knights Hospitallers 23.
Kynebell, Hugh 27.

Lambert 60.
Lambert, John 42, 48, 51, 56, 67.
Lambert, Mary 49, 56.
Lambert, May 56, 79.
Lambert, William 49, 56.
Lamport 66.
Lancaster, Duchy of 47.
Lancaster, Henry of 45.
Langdale 9.
Langetots de 49.
Langland, Dr. 34.
La Tene Culture 9.
Latimer, Lord 70, 71, 72, 73.
Latin School, Royal 26, 35, 63, 96, 116, 117.
Lea River 15.
Leckhampstead 9.
Leeds 104, 116.
Leet Court 75.
Leicester 51, 92, 93.
Lenborough 14, 19, 23, 28, 40, 49, 56, 58, 65.
Lenborough Manor 79.
Lenborough Road 51, 94, 115.

Leofric 16.
Lille 78.
Lillingstone 9.
Lillingstone Lovell 51.
Limerick 65.
Lincoln 19, 28, 34, 40, 41.
Lincoln, Bishop of 20, 22, 26, 28, 32, 91, 92, 96.
Lipscombe 28, 37, 39, 40, 41, 47, 53, 58, 59, 64, 65, 68, 71, 77, 80, 97, 102, 104.
Literary & Scientific Society 112.
Lloyds Bank 73, 98.
Lollards 32, 34.
Lomax, John & Co. 92.
London 25, 61, 62, 63, 69, 73, 74, 79, 92, 102, 115.
London, Bishop of 28.
London Gazette 74.
London Road 94, 98, 102, 111, 114, 117, 119.
London Road Bridge 99, 109.
Long Bridge 99, 109.
Longueville 29.
Lord Lieutenant 103.
Lords Bridge 51, 109.
Louis XIV 74.
Louis XVIII 103.
Lucas, Sir Charles 60.
Luffield 25, 27.
Luke, Sir Samuel 61.
Luton 56.

Madras, Governor of 109.
Magdalen College 32, 91.
Maids Moreton 9, 23, 103, 104, 112.
Maids Moreton Avenue 117.
Maids Moreton House 58.
Manchester 104.
Manchester Ship Canal 98.
Mandeville, William de 45.
Manor House 29, 34, 51, 94, 99.
Marchand, Richard de 22.
Marcier, Richard de 22.
Margaret, Daughter of Llewellyn, Prince of Wales 21.
"Margaret" Ship 54.
Maria, Infanta 55.
Market, Cattle 116.
Market Hill 84, 100.
Market House 106.
Market Square 52, 114, 117, 120.
Markhams 112.
Marlborough, Duke of 78.
Marney, Lord 32.

Marshall, Robert 24, 25.
Mary Charter 107.
Mary, Lady Kinross 113.
Mary of Modena 76.
Mary, Queen 34, 41, 44, 48, 70.
Mary II, Queen 74, 76, 77.
"Mayflower" 54.
McCulloch 110.
Meadowland 49.
Meadway Estate 118.
Mean House 37.
Mercers 52, 53.
Mercia 13, 14.
"Mercurius Aulicus" 60.
Methodist Chapel 117.
Methodist Guild Room 115.
Middleton, Col. 60.
Miller, Mr. 66.
Mill Lane 51, 94.
Mill 119.
Milne House 47.
Milton Keynes 117, 118, 120.
Minshull, Lady 59.
Minshull, Sir Richard 56, 58, 59, 64, 78.
Mitre Street 94.
Mixbury 14.
Monmouth, Duke of 74.
Monmouth Rebellion 76.
Monteage, Stephen 79.
More, Raphael 48.
Moreton, James 34.
Moreton Road 49, 52, 87, 108, 110, 114, 115, 117.
Moulson, Peter 92.
Mount Pleasant 51, 115.
Municipal Corporations Act 107, 108.
Murgelty, Alderman 92.

Naples, Cardinal of 28, 29.
Napoleon III 111.
Napton, Mr. 63, 64.
Narbury 11.
Nash 81.
National Schools 93, 101, 114.
National Westminster Bank 52.
Nelson 94.
Nelson St. 94.
Newcombe, Robert 51.
Newnham, Sir Thomas 35.
Newport Pagnell 27, 60, 61, 62, 70, 72.
Newton Longueville 29.
Newton, Mr. Gabriel 92.
Norburgh, Roger de 26.
Norfolk, Duke of 39.

Normanby, Marquess of 77.
Norris, Rev. W. F. 110.
Northampton 25, 30, 41, 45, 63, 86.
Northampton Mercury 85.
Northamptonshire 41.
North End 85, 86, 94.
North End Court 115.
North End Square 52, 115.
Northumberland, Duke of 34, 41.
Northumbria 13.
Nugent 40, 103.
Nugent, Earl of 103.
Nugent, Mary 103.
Nursing Home 112.

Odd Fellows Hall 115.
Odo, Bishop of Bayeux 19, 20, 49.
Offa, King 15.
Old Change 53.
Old Gaol 52, 108.
Old Latin School 23, 52, 94, 110.
Old Market Hall 101.
Old Stratford 15.
Olney 9, 69.
Osney Abbey 20, 38.
Ouse, Great 10, 11, 12, 13, 15.
Overn Hill Estate 115.
Overn Hill House 87, 115.
Oxford 20, 25, 46, 57, 62, 63, 68, 74, 82, 95.
Oxford University 81, 119.

Padbury 14, 60, 61, 104.
Padbury Brook 10.
Page Hill 9, 117.
Palmer, Miss Alice 110.
Pancake Bell 96.
Parret, River 15.
Passenham 16, 51.
Pate, Richard 34.
Paymaster-General 103.
Pembroke, Earl of 21, 29.
Penda, King 13, 14.
Pepys, Samuel 50.
Perkins, Rev. W. 51.
Peter of the Mill 23.
Petre, Lord 62.
Pevsner, Sir Nickolaus 74, 94.
Picts 13.
Pilgrims Inn 36, 51.
Pillory 101.
Pitt 90.
Plantagenet, Anne 24.
Plantagenet, Humphrey 24.
Plautius, Aulus 10.

Plymouth 54.
Podds Lane 49, 52, 87, 94, 110.
Police Station 108.
Poltrey, Compter 62.
Pomfret, Earl of 39.
Pooley, F. 118.
Pope Clement VII 33.
Post Office 114.
Potter, Thomas 35.
Poulton, Fernando 36.
Poulton, Francis 56.
Praed & Co. 98.
Praed, Mr. 98.
Prebend End 103, 109, 110.
Prebend End Manor 19, 20, 23, 29, 34, 35, 40, 47, 49.
Prebend House 29, 50, 51.
Preston 23.
Preston Bissett 51.
Preston Bissett-cum-Cowley 104.
Primitive Methodist Chapel 110.
Prince of Wales 116.
Purcell, Edward 76, 77.
Purefoy, Col. 58.
Purefoy, Henry 92.
Purefoy, Mr. 58, 92.
Purefoy, Mrs. 98.
Purefoy, William 26.

Quaker's Orchard 110.
Queen Mother 116.

Radclive 51.
Radclive-cum-Chackmore 104.
Railway 109, 116, 120.
"Raisonnable" 94.
Raphael 97.
Ratcliff 69.
Reading Abbey 19, 49.
Red Buildings 86, 89, 94, 101, 112.
Red Cross Show 102.
Redistribution of Seats Act 113.
Reeve, Thomas 35.
Reeve, W. 64.
Reform Bill 103, 104, 105.
Remigius 20.
Rennals, John 69.
Representation of People Act 113.
Resumption, Act of 38.
Reynolds, Peter 69.
Rhineland 9.
Richard I 21, 41.
Richard II 24, 25, 45.

Richard III 22.
Richardson, E. & F. Ltd. 115.
Rickett, Mr. Thomas 111, 116.
Rifle Corps 108.
Roberts, Father 32.
Robinson, Henry 69, 71.
Robinson, William 67, 68, 69.
Robins, George 69.
Rochester 19.
Rogers, John 79.
Rogers, Matthias 79.
Rollo the Viking 17.
Roman Catholic College 111.
Roman-Celtic Temple 12.
Romans 9, 10, 11, 12, 13.
Rome 33, 34, 44, 56.
Rouen 29.
Roundell, Rev. 12, 32, 35, 36, 40, 51, 57, 70, 79, 81, 96, 112.
Royal Bucks Militia 99.
Royal Bucks Yeomanry 99.
Royal Commission 104.
Royal Latin School 79, 116.
Ruding, Archdeacon 23, 36, 80, 110.
Rumbold's Lane 14, 94.
Rumbold's St. Aisle 36, 37.
Rumwold St. 14, 26, 49.
Rupert, Prince 59, 60, 63.

Salcey 10.
Salisbury 31, 45.
Salisbury Plain 9.
Salvation Army 110.
Sandys, Hester 55.
Sansbury, Mr. 87, 88.
Sawle, William 37.
Saxons 13, 16.
School Board 113.
School Lane 10, 93, 112, 114.
Scotland 112.
Scottish Presbyterians 66.
Scott, Rev. Thomas 102.
Scott, Sir G. G. 102, 108, 112.
Secondary School 114, 120.
Selby, Mr. 98.
Selveston, Henry 27.
Serpentine 78.
Sessions House 74, 97.
Seyton, Jonathan 77.
Shaftesbury, Lord 74.
Shalstone 9, 58.
Shalstone Manor House 98.
Shambles 52, 106.
Sharpe, Leonard 63.

Sheffield, John 77.
Sheahan 36, 47, 97, 104.
Shene, Thomas 77.
Sheriff's Bridge 50, 53, 94, 99, 109.
Sheriffs of London 39.
Ship Money 56, 57.
Shoprewe, Le 37.
Sibwine 16.
Sigma Coatings 115, 116.
Silvester 70, 71, 73, 87, 88, 89.
Singleborough 14.
Smith, Col. 60, 61, 62.
Smith, James 52.
Smith, Sir John 55.
Smith, Sir William 70, 71.
Smith, Will 34.
Smythe, Thomas 22.
Snellshall 25.
Snelshall Priory 81.
Society of Friends 110.
Someries 56.
Somerset, Duke of 34.
Somerton, John 26.
Sool, Edward 40.
Southwell, Rev. Henry 32, 34.
Sowerby, Mr. 99.
Spain 55, 90.
Speed, John 50, 46, 94.
Spigurnell, Robert 24.
St. Bartholomew's Hospital 25.
St. Laurence Hospital 22.
St, Thomas Hospital 25.
Stafford, Earl of 21, 24, 45.
Stafford, Edward 32, 54.
Stafford, Henry 30, 31, 41.
Stafford, Humphrey 41.
Stapleton, Sir Philip 60.
Station Road 100, 109.
Steam, Corn & Cake Mills 112.
Steeple Claydon 51.
Stephens, Thomas 35.
Stevens, Will 64.
Stilton, William 64, 68.
Stockholm 16.
Stonehenge 9.
Stony Stratford 60.
Stowe 12, 20, 37, 38, 47, 55, 66, 68, 73
    78, 82, 88, 89, 90, 92, 99, 103, 108, 109,
    113, 116.
Stowe Avenue 99, 114, 116.
Stowe House 90.
Stowe School 116.
Stowe, Vicar of 78.
Stratford Fields Estate 118.

Stratford Road 108, 114.
Stratton, Matthew 34.
Suckling, Capt. 94.
Suene of Rayleigh 45.
Summer Assizes 113.
Summerlee Estate 117.
Sun Insurance Co. 85.
Supremacy, Act of 44.
Surrey, Earl of 38.
Sutton 14, 28.
Sutton, Bishop of Lincoln 36.
Swan & Castle 97.
Swanbourne 59.
Sweyn Forkbeard 16.

Tailors 52, 53.
Tangier 77.
Tanyard 112.
Temples 40, 47.
Temple, Countess 90.
Temple, Earl 90, 96, 97, 103.
Temple, John 55.
Temple, Lord 92.
Temple, Peter 37, 38.
Temple, Richard 90.
Temple, Sir Peter 55, 56, 58, 65, 66.
Temple, Sir Purbeck 90.
Temple, Sir Richard 68, 70, 71, 72, 73, 74,
    77, 78.
Temple, Sir Thomas 55.
Temple, William 90.
Temys, John 37.
Teringham, Thomas 50.
Terrel, Sir Edward 50.
Test Act 76.
Thame 51, 62.
Thame Grammar School 65.
Thames River 15.
Theobalds 56.
Thornborough 14, 104.
Thornborough Bridge 10, 11, 12.
Thornborough Road 94.
Thornton 13.
Thurkytel, Earl 16.
Tingewick 11, 23, 46, 51, 104.
Tingewick Bridge 84.
Tingewick Road 62, 94, 109, 114, 115, 116.
Tingewick Road Bridge 109.
Tingewick Wood 24.
Tipper, William 35.
Tokens 68, 69.
Tostig 17.
Towcester 101.
Tower 66, 67.